ANGER
and
GUILT

ANGER
and
GUILT

Our Foes and Friends

CAROL ROGNE

Outskirts Press, Inc.
Denver, Colorado

The opinions expressed in this manuscript are solely the opinions of the author and do not represent the opinions or thoughts of the publisher. The author has represented and warranted full ownership and/or legal right to publish all the materials in this book.

Anger and Guilt
Our Foes and Friends
All Rights Reserved.
Copyright © 2011 Carol Rogne
V3.0

Cover Photo © 2011 JupiterImages Corporation. All rights reserved - used with permission.

This book may not be reproduced, transmitted, or stored in whole or in part by any means, including graphic, electronic, or mechanical without the express written consent of the publisher except in the case of brief quotations embodied in critical articles and reviews.

Outskirts Press, Inc.
http://www.outskirtspress.com

ISBN: 978-1-4327-7757-9

Outskirts Press and the "OP" logo are trademarks belonging to Outskirts Press, Inc.

PRINTED IN THE UNITED STATES OF AMERICA

Acknowledgement

I am very grateful to Carolyn Solares, who has encouraged me to write in the area of mental health and personal empowerment, based on my experience as a therapist, teacher, and consultant. Carolyn is an inspiration and joy in my life. We share the belief and know that it is a divine blessing that in our lives, there are no limitations, other than the ones we create in our minds. If you are interested in being inspired by this energetic, positive, and creative person, visit her website: carolynsolares.com

Thank you, Carolyn. I love you and am so grateful that you are in my life!

Table of Contents

Introduction ix
Part I: Anger Our Foe and Friend
Chapter 1 3
    The Powerful Emotion of Anger
        Anger is our foe: 17
        Anger is our friend: 18
Chapter 2 21
    Aggressive Anger Used to Control Others
Chapter 3 35
    Working with Our Anger
        Painful childhood experiences 38
        Significant losses in our life 41
        Anger generated within relationships 49
        Anger generated by irrational thoughts and beliefs 63
Chapter 4 73
    Strategies for Working with Anger
Chapter 5 93
    Anger our Friend
Part II: Guilt Our Foe and Friend
Chapter 6 99
    The Powerful Emotion of Guilt
        Guilt is our foe… 109

    Guilt is our friend… 110
Chapter 7 113
    Guilt Used to Control Others
Chapter 8 131
    Responding to Valid Guilt
Chapter 9 141
    Dealing with Irrational Guilt
Chapter 10 159
    Strategies for Working with Guilt
Chapter 11 169
    Guilt Our Friend
Chapter 12 173
    Being Proactive with Anger and Guilt
        I. Focus on prevention and intervention 174
        II. Change irrational thinking 178
        III. Stay in the center 180
Bibliography 183

Introduction

Though the feelings of anger and guilt are part of the human experience, these feelings are often misunderstood. We are bombarded with the violence in all parts of the world, so we naturally think of anger as aggressive anger that is used to control and harm others. However, our anger is a legitimate response when we have been emotionally, mentally, physically, or sexually abused, and can be expressed in appropriate and nonviolent ways. Anger is our friend when it alerts us to harmful situations or faulty ways of thinking that need to be changed. Anger is also a stage in the grieving process, which helps us to emotionally heal when we experience loss.

Guilt is our foe when we accept the false guilt that people project to control us, and when we generate guilt for ourselves by our irrational thinking. However, guilt is our friend when it prompts us to change inappropriate behaviors and make amends when our actions have been harmful or destructive to ourselves and others.

Few of us were taught how to deal with anger, guilt, or other difficult emotions. When we understand more about the feelings of anger and guilt and learn strategies to handle these emotions in positive ways, we are taking major steps in enhancing our emotional, physical, mental, spiritual, and relationship health. We no longer have to experience anger and guilt as enemies that sabotage our life and relationships. Rather, we can embrace these feelings as friends who prompt us to take purposeful actions.

Part I:

Anger — Our Foe and Friend

Chapter 1

The Powerful Emotion of Anger

Emotional health requires acknowledging our natural emotions, including our anger. However, we typically equate anger with aggression and, therefore, tend to view all expressions of anger as harmful and evil. Aggressive anger is so prevalent and destructive that it overshadows how the feeling of anger can be beneficial to us. Most of us have to revise our thinking before we can believe that anger is a healthy emotion that can be our friend.

Anger is a feeling, and feelings are neither good nor bad. Rather, it is how we express our anger that frequently leads to harmful acts against ourselves and others. Although we need to experience our human emotions because they provide information to us, we are socialized in our society to ignore, repress, deny, minimize, and be dishonest about our feelings. We may have learned and still believe that feelings are unimportant, irrational, and unpredictable. However, if we want a healthy emotional life and healthy relationships, we need to develop a healthy relationship with all of our emotions, including anger.

Common views about anger

- ✓ Anger is evil and should not be experienced.
- ✓ Suppressing anger is more virtuous than expressing anger.

- ✓ Religious people don't get angry.
- ✓ Women should not express anger.
- ✓ Adults can be angry, but children should not be angry.

Anger is an emotion that has been problematic for human beings for many centuries, as evidenced by Aristotle's Challenge: *Anyone can become angry—that is easy. But to be angry with the right person, to the right degree, at the right time, for the right purpose and in the right way—that is not easy.*

The feeling of anger is purposeful, and there are legitimate reasons to be angry. Anger is a signal to stop, acknowledge, respect, listen, and reflect on what our anger is communicating to us.

Legitimate reasons to be angry

- Childhood or current physical, sexual, emotional, or mental abuse
- Anger at an abusing parent and the parent who did not protect us from abuse
- Unfairness, dishonesty, inefficiency, propaganda, prejudice, disrespect, and inequities in work, legal, welfare, mental health, religious, medical, or political systems
- Injustice, discrimination, and violation of basic human rights
- Being controlled, harassed, and stripped of personal power
- Anger from hurtful experiences in past relationships
- Having a person be overly dependent on us because they are under-functioning as adults
- Being held hostage in a relationship or job
- Working with under-functioning coworkers and/or supervisors
- Receiving faulty or unnecessarily complicated instructions so success is not possible

- Having our personal space invaded
- Having progress toward goals blocked by controllers
- Being viewed and treated as inferior and inadequate
- Having the criteria for success raised by a controller, just when success is within reach
- Being angry because we are over-extended and doing too many things for too many people
- Feeling angry when people are rude, unfriendly, uncooperative, and negative
- Being punished for our strengths or when speaking out for needed changes

Our healthy anger might prompt us to speak up and confront abuse that we are experiencing. Societal reforms start with the anger that is generated when people experience injustice and oppression. When we use our anger for motivation to create healthy change in ourselves, our relationships, in our communities, and in our world, we are honoring this emotion and working with it in productive ways.

What we learned about anger in our childhood is likely to be the way we express anger in adulthood. Our parents may have carried anger internally and the anger was not expressed, or we may have experienced our parents frequently fighting and yelling at each other or being physically violent. Some of us saw nitpicking, bickering, or cold silence. None of these ways of dealing with anger are emotionally healthy.

When we were children and were angry, we may have been shamed, even though our anger may have been legitimate, and told, "You shouldn't be angry." Young girls are taught in our culture to be nice, passive, and that being angry is unacceptable. Boys are socialized to be competitive, strong, and are often told to physically fight back when challenged. One of the reasons why our adult relationships become dysfunctional is because we learned unhealthy ways of expressing anger in our childhood.

We may have been told to stop feeling angry, or stop feeling any emotion. Few children are invited to share their anger by a parent saying, "You seem angry. Let's talk about why you are angry. Maybe I can help you." Nor were we taught how to embrace and express other feelings in appropriate ways. We may have learned to suppress not only our anger, but our fears, insecurities, and worries. To please our parents and avoid reprimands, we may have never talked about our feelings, least of all anger. Now, as adults, our feelings are ignored and seldom expressed, especially our anger.

- Meghan shares:

    When I was a young child, I was told, "Shame on you!" when I talked about my anger, so I didn't talk about my feelings when I was angry. When I was young, I was lucky, because there weren't too many things that made me angry. But when I was an adult, I experienced anger in my marriage and sometimes at work. I suppressed the anger, thinking something was wrong with me. I tried to keep a lid on my anger. When I had reached my limit, my anger usually came out in tears, but then I would be so upset that I couldn't express what I needed to say and I wasn't taken seriously.

It is not uncommon to behave in ways that are similar to a dysfunctional parent's behavior, but we seldom recognize this and become defensive when someone points out, "Your behaviors are just like your father's…or just like your mother's." Despite our intentions of being totally opposite of a dysfunctional parent, we frequently end up displaying the same behaviors, which is seldom in our awareness, but evident to others.

We can revise our understanding of anger and realize that anger is not the same as aggression and that it is how we express anger that often causes harm to ourselves or others. We can identify the cause of our anger, develop a plan, and take action to correct the situation and express our anger appropriately.

Ways of dealing with anger

Our anger is often fueled by fear, loss, unmet needs, or hurt. When we are angry, we may suppress our anger, be passive, passive-aggressive, assertive, or aggressive. We also deal with our anger differently in different situations. Below is a comparison of the different ways people suppress or express their anger. The healthy expression of anger is the assertive, honest position.

Suppressing anger	**Expressing anger passively or passive-aggressively**	**Expressing anger assertively**	**Expressing anger aggressively**
Anger is suppressed and not acknowledged.	Anger is expressed in ways that are indirect and manipulative.	Anger is communicated in direct, honest, and respectful ways.	Anger is directed outwardly in aggressive ways that harm others verbally or physically.

◄ Anger and Guilt

Suppressing anger

Some of us are forced to suppress our anger because if our anger is expressed, there might be serious consequences, including risking physical safety. But even in less serious situations, we routinely suppress, ignore, or try to escape from our anger by over-working or being involved with addictions or addictive activities. We may be carrying anger from childhood or other relationships in the past which generated emotional pain, but keep our anger within ourselves. Suppressed anger consumes emotional energy and remains in our consciousness. If we check our thoughts, we often brew about recent or past angry-making situations that caused emotional pain. Although we may believe that our suppressed anger does not affect our lives, our anger can lead to resentments, thoughts of revenge, depression, or physical illness.

There are several reasons why we suppress our anger. If we believe that all anger is evil, we hesitate to admit that we are angry. We may not communicate our anger because we do not want to hurt or offend anyone. We suppress, rather than express our anger because we have a fear of being rejected or disliked. People-pleasers often carry suppressed anger because they feel like people are taking advantage of them, despite the fact that pleasers frequently offer their services and others simply accept. Women often suppress their anger because they have been taught that expressing anger is not feminine, that men distance themselves from women who express anger, and that anger, even though it might be expressed appropriately, leads to increased conflict. The message that is often given to women is that "Nice women don't get angry," so they often withdraw and are silent. If women suppress their anger, they are viewed as being cooperative, kind, and virtuous, but they are risking their emotional and physical health.

When we withdraw, ignore, avoid controversial and unpleasant communication, or are almost always compliant when others make demands, we are more than likely suppressing our anger. Suppressing anger is being disrespectful of ourselves. The anger festers within us because we do not stand up for ourselves and confront abusive or negative behaviors directed toward us or our children. If we routinely suppress our anger, we might be setting ourselves up to explode with aggressive anger, or do the opposite and break down and cry. When we do this, our credibility is questioned and the other person often concludes or makes accusations that we are out of control or exaggerating the problem. As a result, there is no resolution of the conflict, and chronic anger bleeds into our emotional life each and every day.

Passive and passive-aggressive expressions of anger

Passive-aggressive expressions of anger are often difficult to identify because they are "under the radar," subtle, and manipulative. Called "sideways" anger, passive-aggressive behavior is intentionally behaving in ways that indirectly communicate disapproval or being upset. Behaviors are designed to get attention or agitate the other person involved. People who are passive-aggressive often feel like they are innocent victims who are treated unfairly and misunderstood. They often cause stress by their indirect and convoluted ways of communicating, which involves distorting and twisting what is being said by the other person.

Typical passive or passive-aggressive expressions of anger:

- Sulking, being testy, moody, impatient, or silent
- Being under-responsible so that others will pick up the slack
- Withdrawing in a way that is meant to be noticed by others
- Letting the other person make the decisions, and then complaining about the outcome

- Acting inert, apathetic, and uncaring
- Manipulating by making others feel guilty
- Procrastinating to get attention or irritate others
- Interrupting others' schedules to get attention
- Being argumentative and aggravating
- Complaining about and criticizing other people but not speaking directly to them
- Deceptively hiding anger by laughing, joking, and saying that "everything is just fine!"
- Teasing and badgering others and claiming that they are just being humorous

These dysfunctional ways of expressing anger sabotage healthy communication and create more anger and emotional distance in significant relationships.

Aggressive expressions of anger

Expressing anger aggressively is often a successful way of getting what we want from others. The behaviors are similar to the temper tantrums of young children wanting their way immediately and are an abusive way of saying, "Pay attention to me!" or "I want my way!" or "You are not meeting my expectations!" If we are aggressive with our anger, there is a danger that our rational mind might be taken over by angry emotions, and we act out of blind rage that is seemingly out of our control.

Aggressive anger may escalate conflicts and result in physical aggression and violence. Or, the other person may cave in and comply. Anger that is routinely expressed aggressively is similar to an addiction. We may experience a temporary "high," but we are repeatedly sabotaging ourselves and the relationships that are often the most important to us. Though aggressive anger is destructive, many people continue to have angry outbursts and overlook the harm they are creating within themselves and within their relationships.

Typical aggressive expressions of anger:

- Being hostile and verbally abusive
- Yelling, screaming, demanding, name-calling, and using profanity
- Bullying and badgering a person who is weaker
- Being disrespectful, dishonest, and defensive
- Being sarcastic and manipulating by claiming that the sarcasm is being humorous
- Dominating, threatening, or intimidating in efforts to control
- Believing that power and force are ways to get things done
- Attempting to win, often at the expense of others
- Taking a superior position by putting the other person down
- Aggressively blaming others to make them feel guilty

Anger that is expressed aggressively demonstrates a lack of emotional maturity. We are angry more frequently and have overly strong reactions to challenging and disappointing situations. One reason for a lack of self-control and emotional immaturity is that using mood-altering substances arrests emotional development. If we started using alcohol or drugs in our adolescent years, we continue to act like many adolescents, who tend to be preoccupied with the self, want their own way immediately, and lack self-control.

There are common gender differences regarding the expression of anger. If women speak aggressively and in a controlling manner, they are often criticized, and their aggressive communication may discredit them as well as their message. In contrast, men who speak in an aggressive way are likely to be attentively listened to, and people are more likely to comply with their demands.

Assertive expressions of anger

Emotional health requires that we express our anger <u>assertively</u>. If we are angry because of what is happening in a relationship, our anger is expressed in honest and respectful ways, using normal voice tones when speaking directly to the person about the specific issue. Because we are in control of ourselves, we do not become defensive, withdraw, or overpower others. We confront with confidence, kindness, and consideration for ourselves and for the other person.

Being assertive starts with acknowledging angry feelings, listening to the information our anger brings to us, and activating anger skills such as:

- Cooling down before engaging in a conflict
- Setting a time and place to meet
- Respecting self and others
- Listening as well as speaking
- Being specific as to the real issue
- Using "I" messages saying, "I think…, I feel…, I fear…, I want…" An "I" statement is speaking about ourselves rather than criticizing, blaming, or making the other person responsible for our feelings or reactions. Defensiveness on the part of the other person is less likely to happen with "I" statements.
- Being open, direct, honest, firm, and kind
- Being committed to working toward a win-win solution
- Taking a time-out if the internal anger or the conversation is escalating
- Refraining from placing guilt on others in order to get compliance
- Being confident and calm

When we are assertive, we are creating the highest probability that positive change will occur. If we have spoken assertively and skillfully, and change does not occur, it forces us to determine whether we can remain in a relationship where true and effective negotiation continually proves to be impossible.

The way we deal with anger affects all aspects of our lives

- **Mental health**. Any emotion that is extreme and expressed in ways that are harmful to ourselves or others becomes problematic. Whether the anger is suppressed or expressed passively, passive-aggressively, or aggressively, it affects our ability to think clearly and rationally and make good decisions. When our mind is constantly thinking angry thoughts, we get trapped in a negative mind-set which sabotages mental health. Anger directed inward toward the self is one of the many causes of depression.
- **Emotional health**. Emotional health is adversely affected when anger is expressed inappropriately:
  - ✓ When we suppress anger, we have less awareness of other feelings.
  - ✓ When we are passive or passive-aggressive in our anger expressions, we are harmful to both ourselves and others.
  - ✓ When we use aggressive anger to control others and make demands, we harm others and create distance in relationships.
  - ✓ When we lash out at others with aggressive anger, we feel guilt and remorse, although these feelings are often suppressed.
  - ✓ Chronically angry people are critical of others because they are critical of themselves, which compromises emotional health.

- ✓ Angry people often believe that they are a victim and that other people, who are believed to be incompetent or insensitive, make their life miserable. Their anger is often excessive and disproportionate to the situation. This negatively affects their emotional health.

- **Physical health**. Suppressing anger is storing the anger within our bodies, and may compromise our physical health. Being aggressively angry is physically distressing to our bodies, creating physical sensations including a racing heartbeat, faster breathing, tense muscles, shaky hands, sweating, a flushed face, heavy energy in the chest and abdominal area, a burning sensation in the stomach, or a lightning bolt piercing the head or chest. Adrenaline and other stress hormones are released. Anger outbursts are stressful to our nervous and cardiovascular systems and can create or exacerbate existing health problems. Suppressed and aggressive anger have been linked to heart disease, elevated blood pressure, high cholesterol, headaches, stomach and intestinal diseases; hormone, respiratory, and skin disorders; cancer and arthritis.
- **Spiritual health**. When anger is suppressed, we are harming <u>ourselves</u>. When anger is aggressively directed outward, our anger is abusive to <u>others</u>. Harming either ourselves or others is contrary to spiritual principles.
- **Relationships**. When we suppress and are silent regarding situations that cause anger, relationships suffer because the anger builds up and serves as a barrier to emotional intimacy. When we express our anger aggressively, others become fearful and often feel like they are forced into compliance, which generates resentments and a desire to escape from the angry, controlling person.

- **Parenting**. Aggressive expressions of anger, combined with the physical size of an adult, are frightening to children. The way that we express our anger is often the way children will express their anger, unless there are other causes, such as mental health issues. Not only does teaching children healthy ways to deal with anger enhance their lives, but when they are adults, they will teach their anger knowledge and skills to the next generation.
- **Work performance and work relationships**. If we have angry outbursts in our work setting, we are likely to be viewed as out of control and unstable. Our inability to handle our anger will sabotage our success as employers or employees.

> Reflecting on my anger:
> The main anger situation I have in my life is:
> I do not allow myself to get angry because:
> If I ever got angry, I would:
> I have anger from the past because:
> I frighten others with my anger when:
> My anger challenge:

Anger and religion

Organized religion frequently implies that anger is un-Christian, immoral, and evil, most likely because anger is viewed as aggressive and harmful to others. However, Jesus was angry because merchants had set up a marketplace in the holy temple. He expressed his anger by overturning tables and his words were, "My temple is a place of prayer, but you have turned it into a den of thieves." He followed the most important rule of anger, that of not hurting oneself

◄ Anger and Guilt

or others. He demonstrated that anger can be used as motivation to confront wrong actions. This must be an important lesson for us because the story is covered in all of the gospels (Matthew 21:12-13, Mark 11:15-18, Luke 19:45-56, John 2: 13-17). Other King James Version scripture passages regarding anger are:

- Ephesians 4:26. "Be ye angry, and sin not: let not the sun go down upon your wrath." This is directing us to express anger, but not in ways that are sinful because of harming others or ourselves. This is also a directive to not harbor our anger within ourselves.
- Colossians 3:21. "Fathers, provoke not your children to anger, lest they be discouraged." This is directing parents to not agitate children with anger because it is emotionally harmful. Children may become discouraged because they are powerless to change the behaviors of parents who express their anger aggressively.

Intensity levels of anger vary

People experience anger with different levels of intensity and express their anger in different ways. Some people have "hot" responses, some "warm," and some "cool" responses to the same situation. We all know of people who become extremely angry, while others stay calm. Reasons for different experiences and expressions of anger include: the level of emotional maturity and self-control, the amount of internal anger within the person, whether old anger is being triggered by a current situation, whether the person has a need to feel superior, right, and control others; and what we learned as children regarding anger. Another factor is that some people have a wide range of emotions, while others are guarded and seldom express their feelings.

Anger is our foe:

- When our anger is emotionally, mentally, physically, and spiritually destructive to ourselves and others
- When the intensity of our anger is not appropriate to the situation, which indicates that we have unresolved past anger
- When we express anger in abusive ways
- When we are in a constant state of anger at ourselves or others
- When we are defensive when given feedback, rather than hearing and acting on valid and truthful information
- When our anger interferes with our rational thinking
- When our angry outbursts expose our lack of self-control
- When our anger sabotages emotional intimacy because it creates fear in others
- When our anger gives us a sense of power over others
- When we feel better by hurting others with our aggressive expressions of anger
- When we are so angry that we make impulsive and negative choices
- When we express our anger aggressively, and situations escalate into physical violence
- When we express anger to get attention, which reveals our lack of maturity
- When we are angry to test the limits in a relationship to see how far we can go without being rejected or abandoned
- When we pattern our angry behaviors after the violence in video games or the media and not only accept, but are entertained by violence

◄ Anger and Guilt

Anger is our friend:

Anger, rather than being an enemy that sabotages our life, can be a beneficial, life-fostering friend. Anger stands ready to provide the motivation to start what we need to start, finish what we need to finish, stop what we need to stop, release what we need to release, confront what we need to confront, clean what we need to clean, repair what we need to repair, move ourselves out of "park" and go forward with our life that we, alone, design.

Our anger can help us change behaviors when we are angry at ourselves for:

- Eating too much
- Not exercising
- Being lazy
- Spending too much money
- Drinking too much alcohol and having another miserable hangover
- Getting a DUI or speeding ticket
- Smoking
- Receiving late fees and/or overdraft charges
- Wasting time
- Caving in to the manipulations of controllers
- Facing consequences that we could have prevented if we were responsible
- Agreeing to do things we don't want to do
- Not starting a recovery process for an addiction
- Not making difficult decisions about our life and moving forward toward our goals

In these and other types of situations, we can listen to anger as a friend, hear the message, and act on it, rather than continually reprimanding ourselves for not taking action. When we listen to our anger regarding these types of behaviors, it is usually obvious what we need to do. If there is a reason that we are unable to act on what our anger is communicating to us, we can access help, such as therapy or a recovery program, a life coach, or support for anxiety or depression.

Other important ways that anger is our friend:

- Anger asks us to stop, listen, pay attention, and speak up about something that needs to change in our lives, such as being emotionally abused in a relationship.
- Anger provides energy and strength to defend ourselves or escape when we are in physical danger.
- Anger provides motivation and energy to escape from an abusive relationship.
- Anger is a stage in the *grieving* process that helps us emotionally recover from loss.
- Anger reminds us that our irrational thinking may be generating unnecessary anger.
- Anger challenges us to identify our controlling and self-serving behaviors.
- Anger alerts us when we create our own anger by having unrealistic expectations of others.
- Anger provides energy that can be directed into creating healthy change.
- When being proactive rather than reactive with our anger, we can use our anger for motivation to make good decisions for ourselves and take positive action.
- Most societal reforms start with the anger energy that is generated when people experience injustice and oppression.
- Anger might send an alarm to us that we have an accumulation

of anger from our childhood because we lived in a dysfunctional home.
- Anger alerts us to problematic issues in our family relationships.
- Anger provides motivation to confront and work for changes or to take an unpopular, but morally right position, despite opposition.

These and possibly other reasons lend support to the belief that anger can truly be a supportive friend who has our best interests in mind. Learning anger skills and dealing with conflict peacefully within our families is an important contribution to achieving peace in our world.

Key Points:

1. Anger is commonly viewed as aggression. However, aggression is only one way of expressing the feeling of anger.
2. Anger is appropriate and valid for many reasons, including childhood or current abuse, and is a stage in the emotional healing process of grieving.
3. Anger is often suppressed, expressed passively, passive-aggressively, or aggressively. However, being assertive is the most effective and respectful way of expressing anger.
4. Anger is our *foe* when we emotionally, mentally, physically, and sexually abuse others.
5. Anger is our *friend* when recognized as a source of information and motivation to make changes in our way of thinking, our behaviors, in our relationships, and in our world.

Chapter 2

Aggressive Anger Used to Control Others

The two most common controlling behaviors are expressing anger aggressively or by making others feel guilty. This involves taking a one-up or one-down power position.

One-up, one-down power positions

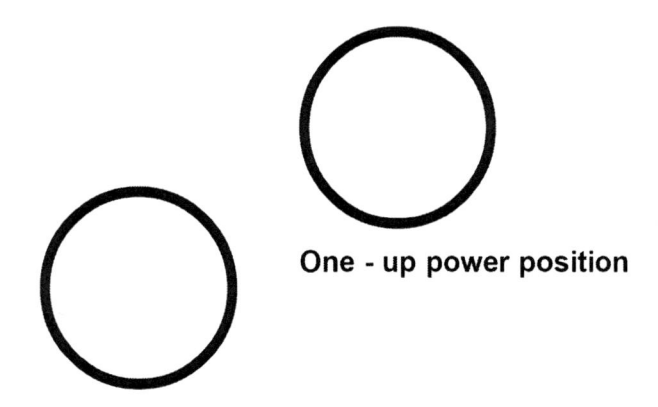

One - up power position

One - down power position

◄ Anger and Guilt

    This diagram illustrates the power positions of one-up and one-down. When one uses a competitive, dichotomous, either-or way of thinking, which controllers often use, there are *two power positions: up or down.* Being aggressively angry, critical, ordering, directing, and commanding are ways of taking a *one-up* position. A *one-down* position is posturing as being helpless or victimized and using guilt or other manipulative tactics to control another person, who often responds out of obligation rather than choice.

Controller takes a one-up position by expressing anger aggressively to get compliance

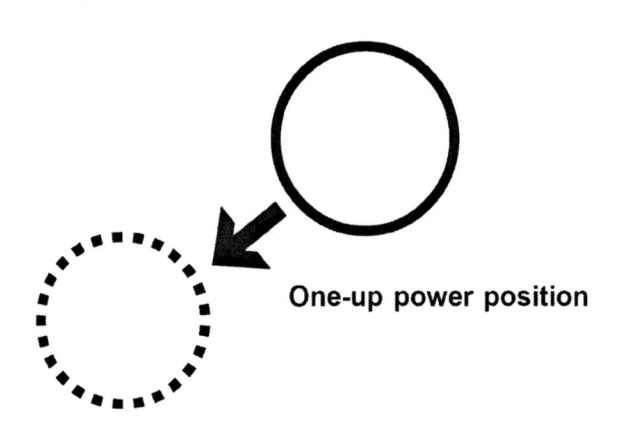

One-up power position

One - down less powerful position

    This diagram illustrates a controller taking a one-up position by being aggressively angry, critical, and demanding. Controlling others with aggressive anger is interpersonally violent. **Violence is any word, look, sign, or action that hurts a person's body,**

◄ 22

possessions, dignity, or security. The controlled person is often forced to comply with the demands of the controller, particularly when there is a potential for violence. Besides creating fear, controllers are often unpredictable. People are rendered more powerless when they cannot predict the situations, topics, ideas, or conversations that will set off a controller's anger outbursts.

Controllers seldom take responsibility for the behavior that is interpersonally violent. Some people enjoy the physical "rush" of energy that anger provides and actually seek the physical sensation, which is behavior that resembles addiction. Controllers enjoy the thrill of winning when people comply with their demands. However, like any addiction, controllers' anger creates problems in one or more areas of their life and is highly stressful and exhausting to others.

Besides being demanding, controllers are often sarcastic, which is a way that anger is expressed indirectly as a way of taking a one-up power position. Sarcastic individuals often have high levels of internal anger and temporarily feel better by making others feel badly through insults, threats, or disrespectful name-calling. Often, sarcastic comments are claimed to be *teasing* by the controller. If their victims react with anger or hurt, they will say, "What's the matter? Can't you take a joke?" Or, "Don't be so sensitive. I was only kidding." By manipulating in this way, they claim innocence of any harmful actions.

Many controllers become intensely angry more often than other people. Underlying controllers' anger and defensiveness is fear, insecurity, and a competitive way of thinking. Thinking competitively requires being right, winning, and being superior. To maintain this superior position, controllers use aggressive anger to create fear, are often dishonest, and discount or negate the thoughts and feelings of others. As a result, they experience chronic tension, stress, and distance in relationships.

People who are controlled are put in a one-down position and comply, agree, and enable the aggressive behaviors to avoid conflict and to protect themselves and their children. If the aggressive anger is confronted, the controller often escalates the anger, makes excuses, or blames others. Even though controllers may want to change their angry, controlling behaviors, it is difficult to change behaviors that have been successful in getting people to do what controllers want them to do. Aggressive anger is efficient because people often respond quickly to demands because they are fearful, whereas negotiating and compromising are more time-consuming and require more skills.

Controllers often become aggressively angry when they are:

- Not the center of attention, ignored, or rejected
- Treated unfairly, whether it is real or perceived
- Challenged or criticized
- Frustrated because of losing or being inconvenienced
- Challenged by different opinions
- Given advice
- Met with resistance to requests

Family members are often the *target* of the controller's aggressive anger, but they are usually not the *real cause* of the anger. What controllers seldom realize is that they run the risk of their children, when they are older, returning the aggressive anger in retaliation. Or, significant people are likely to abandon the controller, which is a natural response to being controlled.

Anger expressed aggressively in efforts to control others may:

- ✓ Scare other people into submission
- ✓ Create an adrenaline rush
- ✓ Provide a sense of power

- ✓ Provide excitement and relieve boredom
- ✓ Make people listen
- ✓ Hide emotional vulnerability
- ✓ Be a way of avoiding feelings of inadequacy or fear
- ✓ Establish superiority over others
- ✓ Be a manipulative way to present the self as powerful and strong

When anger is expressed aggressively, combined with the power that comes with physical size, strength, and being of the male gender, it often feels like there is a potential for being harmed and, therefore, persons are willing to appease the controller by being compliant.

The abuse cycle is fueled by aggressive anger

Aggressive ways of expressing anger are emotionally and mentally harmful and can lead to physical abuse, which has the following stages:

- ➤ The tension-building stage: The angry person becomes increasingly agitated. As tension and control increase, the partner attempts to pacify or please the abuser in order to prevent conflict. Despite these actions, criticism and anger escalate.
- ➤ The abuse stage: A trivial event often triggers the abuse. The victim is often blamed and frequently accepts the blame.
- ➤ The remorse stage: After the abuse, the abuser apologizes and makes promises to never abuse again. The more codependent and insecure the partner, the more vulnerable they are to the partner's persuasions.
- ➤ The honeymoon stage: Everything seems calm and normal and the abuser may temporarily stop being verbally or

Anger and Guilt

physically abusive, but soon the perpetrator starts becoming angry again, and the abuse cycle returns to the tension-building stage. As the relationship progresses, the abuse typically escalates, and the length of the honeymoon stage decreases.

The abuse cycle is a result of extremely aggressive expressions of anger. Both the perpetrator and the victim need professional help.

How is my anger used to control others?

Why do I feel the need to control?

What effect does my controlling behavior have on my relationships?

How did my parents express anger?

How did their ways of expressing anger affect me?

Who are the people that experience my anger?

Am I experiencing the abuse cycle as either a perpetrator or a victim?

My anger challenge:

When we need professional help with our anger

We harm ourselves, as well as others, with aggressive anger. There are biochemical changes in our bodies when we rage, use profanity, or threaten and intimidate others. People who express their anger aggressively have more health problems, such as high blood pressure and heart attacks. The following are indicators of needing professional help with anger:

- When angry, we are too intense and get in loud arguments and physical fights routinely.
- Our anger lasts too long and we experience high levels of stress.
- We verbally abuse others and often use profanity when angry.
- We frighten our children and spouse with our angry outbursts.
- We have intense anger over past experiences.
- We are frequently aggressive and out of control with our anger.
- We are known as a "hot-head" by several people.
- We are angry and irritable most of the time.
- We make problems larger than they are, which increases the level of our anger.
- We are excessively and frequently angry at *ourselves.*
- We have lost relationships because of our anger.
- We demand that we have our way, even if it means intimidating or abusing others.
- We cannot function at a job because of our anger.
- We become angry at situations and issues that others view as trivial.
- We have had legal consequences because of anger.
- Friends avoid us because of our anger.

- ✓ We are fearful of our own anger and how our anger harms others.
- ✓ We want to harm ourselves.

Reasons why I need professional help with my anger:

My action plan:

Aggressive anger used to control is often enabled

Recipients of control—often minority groups, women, or people living under abusive dictatorships—experience legitimate anger because their rights are taken away by more powerful, controlling people. When the control is life-threatening, people who are controlled are often *forced to enable* the control that is oppressing them in order to keep themselves and their children safe. *Confronting* those who are controlling and oppressing us with aggressive anger is often a risk that cannot be taken.

Even though we may live with controlling persons who do not threaten our physical safety, we often enable angry, controlling behaviors as a way to prevent conflict and/or to protect ourselves and our children from emotional abuse. We also comply with a controller's requests because we don't want to be viewed as someone who creates hassles or is mean and selfish, which are often the manipulative accusations made by controllers. Enabling stems from good intentions but results in helping the controller to be successful in their controlling behaviors. It is like buying alcohol for the alcoholic, calling their workplace to report their illness when it is actually a hangover, and cleaning up their messes. Our enabling allows the controller to avoid the consequences of dysfunctional and abusive actions. When we enable, we allow, accommodate, adjust, comply, protect, sacrifice preferences and dreams, and pretend that everything is fine when everything is not fine.

Enabling includes the following behaviors:

Allowing **is enabling controlling, aggressive anger**:

- ✓ Being silent when our children are routinely verbally attacked and unjustly criticized
- ✓ Failing to recognize that permitting is promoting the controlling behaviors
- ✓ Going along to get along

Accommodating **is enabling controlling, aggressive anger**:

- ✓ Changing plans to prevent anger
- ✓ Lowering valid expectations regarding the relationship
- ✓ Trying to meet the controller's numerous expectations so the controller does not get angry
- ✓ Being dishonest to prevent conflict
- ✓ Agreeing and aligning with a controller's decisions, even if we know they are wrong
- ✓ Internalizing the controller's anger and guilt statements

Adjusting **is enabling controlling, aggressive anger**:

- ✓ Trying to be, do, think, feel and behave according to what the controller wants
- ✓ Changing personal preferences and interests to match the controller's preferences and interests to prevent anger

- ✓ Praising the controller's positive behaviors that should be *expected* in relationships, such as saying, "Thank you for being nice to me."
- ✓ Being compliant, passive, and not standing up for what we believe in, attempting to prevent the controller's anger

***Complying* is enabling controlling, aggressive anger**:

- ✓ Doing everything that the controller wants us to do to pacify her/him
- ✓ Being compliant to prevent, avoid, or stop an angry outburst
- ✓ Trying to do things perfectly to avoid the controller's anger
- ✓ Saying "yes" when we really want to say "no"
- ✓ Teaching children to be compliant so a parent doesn't become angry
- ✓ Agreeing to participate in disliked or uninteresting activities to prevent aggressive anger outbursts

***Protecting* is enabling controlling, aggressive anger**:

- ✓ Not discussing family problems with trusted others outside of the family to prevent the controller's anger
- ✓ Trying to keep children quiet so the controller doesn't get angry
- ✓ Not talking about anything controversial
- ✓ Not upsetting or irritating the controller to prevent anger
- ✓ Minimizing the emotional damage that is being created by the controller's anger
- ✓ Confronting the angry behaviors but then retracting what is said
- ✓ Not confronting angry behaviors
- ✓ Making excuses to oneself, children, or others, for the

controller's aggressive anger

Sacrificing **preferences and dreams is enabling controlling, aggressive anger**:

- ✓ Placing more importance on the controller's preferences and dreams than our own to prevent anger
- ✓ Not actualizing our life regarding our work or personal development to avoid the controller's anger

Pretending **that everything is fine when everything is not fine is enabling controlling, aggressive anger**:

- ✓ Crying but insisting that nothing is wrong because the controller may become upset or may ridicule us
- ✓ Pretending to be okay when in emotional pain
- ✓ Saying that we are not angry when we really are angry to prevent more conflict
- ✓ "Psyching up" to be nice, pleasing, and tolerant of the angry, self-serving, and controlling behaviors

Enabling dysfunctional or controlling behaviors may have begun in childhood. These were our best efforts to prevent angry or disapproving responses from parents, to be accepted and loved, or sometimes, to survive. When we were children, enabling played out in different ways. Some of us tried to be the perfect child to please parents and are now trying to please an angry partner. Many of us became an overly self-sufficient child, and we are now over-functioning in a relationship. Being good, quiet, or invisible may have been our attempts to prevent a parent's anger. Giving up our old ways of handling angry behaviors directed toward us is difficult, because we have lived with our self-designed and unique ways of

◀ Anger and Guilt

enabling for a long time. Part of our personal empowerment will be identifying the ways that we allow, enable, and give our power away when we are experiencing being controlled with aggressive anger.

- Mary shares:

    I was fearful of his anger and I didn't want it to get worse, so I would go along with whatever he said, especially when our children were around. I felt I had no choice. When he would get upset and angry, we were scared and tried to do what he wanted. But we never knew what was going to trigger his anger. Whatever we did for him, we could never do it good enough.

How do I enable the aggressive anger that is used to control?

Why do I enable these behaviors?

My anger challenge:

Responding to one-up, one-down manipulative, controlling tactics

Controllers who use one-up, one-down tactics overlook the fact that there is a neutral, middle, assertive position that is increasingly being understood and used by people who refuse to be manipulated. If the control does not carry the threat of personal harm, one can respond to the controller by taking a neutral position, rather than being manipulated by a one-up statement. As a result, controllers are often unsure of what to do because their control maneuvers are not working.

Aggressive Anger Used to Control Others

The following is a one-up, one-down scenario:

Controller A: "You never want to do what I want to do! What is wrong with you?" (This is a one-up statement to establish a superior, one-up position.)
Person B: "I don't have the same interests as you do." (This is an assertive statement. Person B is not manipulated into a one-down position.)
Controller A: "I know. You are so odd!" (Another one-up statement.)
Person B: "I just don't have the same interests as you do." (Person B is taking an assertive position and repeating what was previously said.)
Controller A: "Well, I just don't understand how you think. You are so selfish!" (This is a one-up statement, meant to manipulate Person B.)
Person B: "I just don't have the same interests as you do. You have a right to think what you think." (Person B does not retract the statement.)

The outcome of this communication is that the controller did not succeed in putting Person B in a one-down position. Person B did not give away his/her power and was not manipulated by Controller A.

Key Points:

1. One of the most common ways of controlling others is the aggressive expression of anger.
2. Violence is any word, look, sign, or action that hurts a person's body, possessions, dignity, or security.
3. Sarcasm is anger communicated indirectly and often manipulatively disguised as humor, with the intention of being one-up, superior, and more powerful.

4. The abuse cycle is a result of extremely aggressive expressions of anger. Both the perpetrator and the victim need professional help.
5. We often enable angry, controlling behaviors as a way to prevent angry outbursts and/or protect ourselves and our children.

Chapter 3

Working with Our Anger

Anger can be a very intense emotion that can be overwhelming at times. Because of this, we may try to *avoid* our anger. However, there are many benefits in learning how to handle this difficult emotion. A mistake we often make is bringing our childhood or past anger issues into current relationships. If we separate and work through our past anger, we are less likely to over-react when challenging situations arise in family or other relationships.

Working with our anger may be the last thing that we want to do because:

- We are aware of our anger, but do not know how to work with our angry feelings.
- We suppress our anger because we think anger is evil. We may have been told as children that we should not be angry. Because we learned that anger is a negative and a forbidden feeling, we act like we are never angry and feel guilty if we express anger.
- We are terrified at the thought of acknowledging our anger, thinking that it might totally consume us.
- We think we have forgotten our past emotional pain and that it is not affecting our current emotional life or our relationships.

- We are not aware that the emotional healing process of grieving involves working with our anger.
- We think our internal anger is only because of current relationship problems.
- We have built internal emotional walls for self-protection, and behind our walls, we carry suppressed, internal anger.
- We think that dealing with our anger is going to be too difficult and emotionally painful.
- We are uncertain as to whether working through our anger will be beneficial.

Despite our hesitations to work with our anger, there are many benefits to becoming clear on its sources, reducing the amount of anger that we generate by our irrational thoughts, releasing the anger we have been harboring, and confronting, when possible, the person who uses anger to control us.

Becoming angry is a process

Though being angry seems like something that instantaneously happens *to* us because people *make us* feel angry, becoming and being angry is a process that is usually out of our conscious awareness. The sequence of becoming angry is:

1. A situation or event occurs.
2. Our thoughts and beliefs create our perception of the situation.
3. Our perceptions of the event create our feelings.
4. Our perceptions and feelings about the event influence whether we become angry, the intensity of our anger, and the ways that we express the anger.

Working with Our Anger

The reality is that we are not born with our thoughts or beliefs that influence our perceptions. We learned them. Not all of our thoughts or beliefs are healthy or useful. Some may be harmful, such as thinking, "I have a right to control others." Or, "I am always a victim." Or, "I must get my way or I am totally defeated." Since our thoughts create our reality, we may be *making ourselves angry,* or our anger may be exaggerated and disproportionate to the situation. When our thoughts and beliefs are dysfunctional, challenging situations are made even more difficult and generate more anger.

Because of different thoughts, beliefs, perceptions, and emotions, people respond to situations differently. To a sarcastic comment, some people will walk away and forget it, while others will take offense, become angry, and escalate the situation or hold a grudge for a long time. As we emotionally mature and learn anger skills, we don't flare up over what other people would view as trivial. In addition, we don't work ourselves up to an agitated and angry state, which increases the chances of making poor choices with our anger. All too often people will report that their temper consumed them, they didn't know what they were doing, and their blind rage led them to become physically aggressive with a spouse, child, or a person who was confronting or challenging.

Mature adults come to the realization that external factors, such as people, situations, and experiences, are not the cause of our emotions. It is our thoughts and beliefs regarding the situations or experiences that create our emotions and generate either positive or negative behaviors. We can choose to be angry, yell, and slam doors. Or, we can choose to be more rational and, if the other person is willing, talk things out. How we think and feel about a situation influences whether we choose to respond appropriately or inappropriately; ineffectively or effectively; abusively or respectfully.

The recipients of our most dysfunctional angry behaviors are usually the people we claim to love the most. They may experience behaviors that we would never let other people see. The fact is that the closest person to our self is our own self. If we have anger at our self, we often project our anger onto others. Nobody enjoys rejection. However, our angry statements and actions can set us up for exactly what we do not want. People eventually avoid us if we are routinely angry, behave in ways to get constant attention, are preoccupied with self, or are frequently complaining. If our thought is, "I am alone, and nobody loves me," the pattern is often to continue the behaviors that cause rejection, which sabotages what we are really craving, which is attention and love. When our behaviors improve, people naturally respond more positively toward us.

Our anger has many sources, including:

- Painful childhood experiences
- Significant losses in our life
- Anger generated within relationships
- Anger generated by irrational thoughts and beliefs

Painful childhood experiences

When living with chronic family of origin dysfunction, a legitimate feeling is anger, which is often suppressed or, on the other extreme, expressed aggressively. This anger is often carried into our adult lives and involves painful childhood experiences including:

- Physical, sexual, emotional, and mental abuse
- The temporary or permanent loss of a significant person through death, divorce, deployment, prison, or other causes
- Excessive parental control
- Unmet physical, emotional, mental, or social needs

- Emotional abandonment due to parental addictions, mental illness, or other causes
- Living in fear because parents often expressed their anger aggressively
- Not being able to escape the abuse or protect a parent or siblings from the abuse
- Other painful experiences in our childhood, such as being bullied, excluded, or being the subject of ridicule and rumors

Painful childhood experiences are usually a result of one or more family members being dysfunctional and often involve inappropriate expressions of anger. Family-of-origin dysfunction is caused by dynamics within a family that limit the emotional, social, mental or spiritual development of family members. We are all different in the degree of the dysfunction experienced in our childhoods. Some of us experienced minimal family dysfunction, while others have had abusive experiences that are emotionally as painful as physically walking through fire. One or both parents may have been in an active addiction process. Our parents may have been divorced, our daily routines chaotic and unpredictable, and we may have felt emotionally torn between our parents. Some parents provide for their children's physical needs but neglect their emotional needs. Some of us had controlling, verbally abusive parents who criticized us for making simple mistakes, our appearance, or our personality characteristics. If we had parents who were physically and/or sexually abusive, we may have lived in fear every day and cannot remember ever feeling safe.

All of us are in need of some type of healing from our childhoods. We may strongly resist the thought of recalling, acknowledging, and processing our painful feelings that originated in our childhood. Some child abuse is so horrendous that we block our memories to survive and cannot recall what happened to us as

Anger and Guilt

children. Or, we may have been minimizing our painful experiences in childhood in order to function in our lives. It is often around the age of thirty when painful childhood memories become obtrusive and persistent. Our healing will involve opening ourselves up to our memories and recalling what actually happened. We will probably experience anger and sadness, which are part of the grieving process, and during this journey and all of its emotional pain, we need to love and nurture ourselves.

When we live in dysfunctional families as children, the parental pattern is often repeated, despite resolutions to be different. We may grow up expressing our anger aggressively and become physically violent, which traumatizes people and relationships.

- Mel shares:

    In my family, there was so much chaos and anger that I spent a lot of time in the barn. I loved the animals and they loved me. In the house, my dad would often be screaming, and I was afraid that he would hurt my mother, and a few times he came close to hitting or choking her. My sisters were also scared of him and spent a lot of time at their friends' house. Our neighbors knew how bad it was in our family and would let us go to their house. I built up so much anger at my dad, and when I got older, I felt like I had turned into my dad. I would wake up angry and little things would set me off. I scared my wife and kids, who ended up leaving me. I got sent to an anger class by my boss and that helped. But I still feel the anger inside of me on most days.

- Brad shares:

    After nearly being arrested and going to jail for attacking my friend, I decided to get some help with my anger. The therapist asked me what the anger was about and I knew immediately. My older brother sexually abused me from the time I was six years old until I was around twelve years old. I hate him to this day, and I hate my mom for letting me be alone with him and not listening to me. Nobody heard me! Just talking about it really helped, but I still felt like my anger was consuming me. I thought a long time about how I could release my anger without taking it out on people and came up with a strategy that worked for me. I always have a chain in my work truck, and I would stop along the road, take my chain, and go into the woods. I would beat the ground and scream out my anger. Sometimes I heard myself sound like a dying animal because of the grief and despair I felt. I would often end by falling down on the ground and praying that I would be released from my anger, which has been with me since I can remember. It took about two years of doing this, but I knew it was helping me because I had fewer times of being out of control with my anger.

Significant losses in our life

Grieving significant losses in our life involves working through the anger stage of the grieving process. Our losses may be:

- ➢ Significant losses in childhood, such as the death of a parent, sibling, or grandparent
- ➢ The death of a child
- ➢ The loss of a partner or spouse through death or divorce
- ➢ The loss we feel when our child has physical, emotional, or behavioral disabilities
- ➢ The loss of employment

◄ Anger and Guilt

- The loss of friends who relocate
- The deterioration or loss of a significant relationship because of dysfunction or abuse
- Compromised health, which may involve loss of physical mobility, sight, hearing, and independent living
- The loss of a chemical or addictive activity when starting a recovery process
- The loss of financial security
- The loss of a happy childhood because of family dysfunction
- The loss of work roles when retiring

The grieving process

Whether our losses are in our adult life or painful experiences in our childhood, our emotional healing involves working through the stages of grief, which are denial, anger, bargaining, depression, and acceptance. All of the emotional stages and feelings are natural to us, but if we ignore or suppress our feelings, or are abusing chemicals, the healing process of grieving is hindered or arrested. Unresolved grief is linked to emotional and physical illness.

The following is a description of the grieving stages. We may want to reach out for support during our grieving by participating in a support group or working with a therapist or clergy, especially if our loss was traumatic and severely affected our lives.

Stage 1: Denial. Denial is meant to give us time to deal with a shock or loss. It is an emotional stage that is meant to be temporary, but some people stay in denial for a long period of time. Staying in denial is often a way of avoiding feelings. When we stay in denial, there are certain behaviors that are common, including:

- Focusing on others to avoid feelings

- ✓ Over-working, over-eating, over-spending
- ✓ Withdrawing from other people
- ✓ Exhaustive physical exercise
- ✓ Fun and pleasure-seeking to avoid feelings
- ✓ Putting on a facade that everything is fine
- ✓ Playing false roles, such as being strong, happy, or courageous
- ✓ Abusing chemicals
- ✓ Blocking memories
- ✓ Blaming others

When we move out of denial, we will naturally move into the next stage, which is anger.

Stage 2: Anger. The second stage of grieving involves anger. When we become aware that anger is part of a healing process, we may be surprised because it seems strange that our anger can help us to emotionally recover from losses. We may be hesitant to work through the anger if we have learned and now believe that anger is evil, not Christian, or if we equate anger with aggressive anger. Some people have a difficult time acknowledging their anger. They describe their feelings as being hurt, rather than being angry. Feeling hurt is more acceptable to them than feeling angry.

When we realize the importance of anger in the grieving process, we are more willing to acknowledge and work with this emotion. Reasons for grief-anger include being angry because a person has left us, being angry at doctors, spouses, siblings, parents, the reality of mortality, angry because there are no answers to our questions, angry because we were abused as children, or angry at God. We may have our own unique reasons for being angry. Some of our anger may be irrational or misdirected, but "our anger is our anger" in this stage of grieving. We do not need to justify our anger, but we do need to deal with it in healthy ways, like choosing to refrain from

◄ Anger and Guilt

aggressively reprimanding someone for something that could not be changed. Our anger will vary in intensity, depending on our loss.

Journaling helps to put words on our feelings. Walking and pondering may be helpful as we process our loss. Verbalizing our anger and other feelings in private, combined with body movement, is effective when working with our anger. As our culture has evolved, we have lost some of our natural physical anger outlets, like beating rugs, digging potatoes, pitching hay, or walking miles to the nearest town. As a result, we have to create our own ways to effectively release our anger. We can also transform the anger energy into creative projects or use the energy for helping others. Meditation is helpful, as is visualizing our anger leaving our minds and bodies. When we are working with our anger, the rule is that we cannot hurt ourselves or others. We cannot internalize our anger and hurt ourselves or lash out at others, which is not helpful in diminishing our anger. More anger strategies are presented in a later chapter.

Working through anger can feel very frightening. However, we can go slow and trust our healing process. If we are grieving painful experiences in our childhood, we do not want to minimize the harm we experienced, but rather, we need to feel the full intensity of the anger. We may reach an emotional place where we feel like we are in the bottom of a pit of anger and despair. We may go into a deep emotional process and cry out in our agonizing, emotional pain, but as we work with our anger, the angry feelings slowly subside, giving us some emotional relief.

If we avoid the anger stage, we may find ourselves:

- ✓ Withdrawing into work
- ✓ Abusing chemicals
- ✓ Compulsively involved in activities
- ✓ Losing control of our anger over trivial things
- ✓ Projecting the anger on innocent persons

- ✓ Being sarcastic and negative
- ✓ Forcing ourselves to act okay
- ✓ Having physical symptoms such as tense muscles, ulcers, chest pains, headaches, respiratory difficulties, or grinding our teeth
- ✓ Having emotional problems such as depression and anxiety

Stage 3: Bargaining. Bargaining is wondering what we *could* have done, or what we *should* have done in the particular situation. In this stage, some people take on too much responsibility and generate a lot of guilt because they expect themselves to be able to do things that are beyond their control, such as not being able to take away someone's pain, not being able to change family dysfunction, or not being with a person at the exact time of death.

When we are healing from childhood wounds, this stage can be used as a perspective-taking stage. We can try to understand the experiences of whoever was abusive or neglectful. However, we do not want to make excuses for the abuse by thinking, "My father was emotionally abusive, *but* his father was the same way, so I shouldn't be angry." Perspective-taking is not protecting, minimizing, or excusing the abusive behavior that we experienced. As a child, regardless of our behaviors, we did not deserve any type of abuse. If we are grieving adverse experiences in our childhood, these questions may be helpful:

- Did the abusive person grow up in an abusing family?

- Was he/she struggling with an addiction?

- Did she/he have intense levels of anger from childhood?

◄ Anger and Guilt

Thinking about the background of the abusive person may help us to understand the abuse that we experienced. We may choose to forgive, but we do not need to make excuses for abusive behaviors.

Stage 4: Depression. The fourth stage in the grieving process is depression. This involves feeling sad, disconnected with parts of self, unmotivated, and lifeless. The experience of depression is evident in such symptoms as:

- ✓ Extended periods of crying
- ✓ Withdrawing from others
- ✓ Loss of interest in work or hobbies
- ✓ Over-sleeping or insomnia
- ✓ Loss or gain of appetite
- ✓ Drawn facial lines
- ✓ Feelings of being surrounded by a dark cloud
- ✓ Lack of motivation
- ✓ Difficulty in doing daily routines and tasks
- ✓ Feeling that *everything* is very difficult to do
- ✓ Feeling hopeless, helpless, and despairing

Journaling can be very helpful during the stage of depression, and it is a good way to stay active in our grieving process, rather than trying to avoid our depression by distracting ourselves from our healing process.

Stage 5: Acceptance. The final stage of grieving is acknowledging and accepting our loss, along with all of the emotions we experienced. We accept the fact that we cannot change the past and start to move on with our life. We may feel:

- ✓ A feeling of peace
- ✓ Appreciation of what we *do* have
- ✓ Enjoyment of each new day
- ✓ A positive focus about life
- ✓ Increased sensitivity toward others
- ✓ Motivated to reach out to others in emotional pain

The grieving process can be emotionally intense. It is best to take as much time as we need in each stage. However, we can't let ourselves become stalled in a grief stage for a long period of time. We need to keep moving at our own pace. How long it takes a person to even consider acceptance of what has happened depends on the person and the severity of the abuse or loss. Some losses are so severe and traumatic, it can take years to work through the pain, and some of the pain may always be with us. Though there may always be sadness, the time comes when people feel they have worked through the grief to the point of being able to slowly resume their life.

Forgiveness

When we are grieving past abuse, neglect, abandonment, or other harmful actions that we experienced, forgiveness of our offenders is necessary for our emotional healing. When we are unwilling to forgive, we continue to live with anger, resentments, and bitterness. This means that the person who we feel has harmed us still has power over us. We are more able to forgive when we have worked through the difficult emotions that are involved in the grieving process. Our forgiveness of those who negatively impacted our life can mean emotional freedom, which results in enhanced mental, emotional, physical, and spiritual health. We know that we have truly forgiven when we have no negative emotional reaction upon encountering or having passing thoughts about the person. It is like meeting a stranger that we are able to greet pleasantly. We have reached the point of blessed indifference.

Letting Go

Letting go involves releasing a person, a painful experience, our control over someone, or emotionally letting go of someone who has died or who no longer wants to be with us. Throughout our lives, we will be faced with the emotional challenge of letting go, which is more difficult if we struggle with codependency, insecurities, and low self-esteem. The alternative to letting go is feeling continued emotional pain. Whatever the circumstance, letting go is often very difficult. As our letting-go process moves forward, there will be a time when we realize that we *will* survive. Our heart and our spirit will heal. We will somehow be able to pick up the pieces of life, put them back together, and move on with our lives in the best way that we can.

Reflecting:

What experiences or losses do I need to grieve?

Who are the persons involved?

We are all unique in the depth of our emotional wounds, but we are all in need of healing. Making a commitment to do whatever it takes to recover is respecting and taking care of ourselves. We will know that we are on the right path when we are learning to love ourselves, are experiencing more peaceful days, and are reaching out to others in love and kindness.

- Melissa shares:

    My mother died when I was seven after being ill for a short time. My world just crashed. I think the only way I got through the next years was because of my aunt, who was always there for me. Our dad got married, so then we had a new mother. But she just wasn't my real mother! I tried so hard to be good and be nice to her, but my anger came out in all the wrong ways, like being disrespectful and stubborn. I got scolded a lot from my dad. I felt that nobody understood me and that I was a bad person. Later, I met two friends and they listened when I shared about my mom and step-mom, and we would hang out. That was the first time that I thought that somebody cared and listened to me. They helped me a lot during my teenage years, and we are still friends.

Anger generated within relationships

Anger is an emotion that gives notice that abusive or insensitive acts have no place in any relationship. Anger can be a motivating energy to stand up for what is right and good, and clearly state that we expect to be treated respectfully, keeping in mind that we cannot expect from others what we are not giving them. Because actions by one person affect the other person, we are emotionally involved and spend more time with each other; we may experience anger more frequently with our spouses, children, or other family members. We may suppress our anger and withdraw, give others the silent treatment, or appear to be fine on the outside but seethe with anger on the inside. Or, we may express our anger aggressively and be overly critical and sarcastic. In the privacy of our homes, we may have less self-control. Bickering between partners frequently leads to emotional explosions.

When anger is suppressed, expressed passively, passive-aggressively, or aggressively, relationships become more disconnected. Aggressive anger poisons close relationships by creating fear, lowered self-esteem, distance, and more anger. When conflicts are not discussed reasonably and rationally, the relationship has a high probability of collapsing.

Relationship issues that generate anger

- ✓ Power used to control a partner and/or other family members
- ✓ Inappropriate and abusive verbal statements
- ✓ Inappropriate and abusive physical behaviors
- ✓ Money
- ✓ Sex
- ✓ Infidelity
- ✓ Division of household and financial responsibilities
- ✓ Parenting
- ✓ In-laws

When dealing with these issues, few of us have learned appropriate, effective, and respectful ways of communicating our anger that strengthen rather than fragment our relationships.

> How is anger expressed in our family?
>
> Do I express anger to control others?
>
> What happens to my relationships when I express my anger aggressively?
>
> When I suppress my anger and give family members the silent treatment, what happens?

Solving relationship problems assertively

When we are assertive, anger is communicated in direct and honest ways. We are respectful to both ourselves and others in all types of situations. We can make requests, give directions, confront, or provide information in an assertive way. When we experience controlling behaviors directed toward us, we can make statements clearly, firmly, and directly, such as "No!" or, "What you just said is verbally abusive." Or, "Please stop badgering me." It may be a challenge for us to actually communicate these simple statements without taking them back, apologizing for saying them, or feeling guilty because our controller chooses to have hurt feelings when faced with the truth.

The basics of being assertive:

- Set a time and place to speak to the other person.
- Rehearse in your mind or write down what needs to be said. You can also think about possible responses by the other person and mentally prepare assertive responses in return.

◄ Anger and Guilt

- Communicate in a neutral, middle power position rather than a superior, one-up, aggressive position; or an inferior, one-down, passive position.
- Start sentences with "I," rather than "You," to avoid blaming statements.
- Be honest, respectful, firm, but kind, and speak in normal voice tones.
- Listen without interrupting.
- Be specific about the behavior that is offensive to you by speaking clearly, rather than expecting the person to "get the drift."
- Use short sentences when confronting.
- Resist the temptation to end the conversation because of emotional discomfort.
- Stick to the specifics of the current situation, rather than bringing up past hurts.
- Repeat the original statement if the other person becomes defensive, starts discounting what is being said, or changes the topic.
- Go slowly and pay attention to what is happening in the communication process.
- Take a time-out if an eruption of anger is imminent.
- Practice calming inner self-talk.
- Being assertive also means affirming others. Thank the person for listening and for her/his time.

Communication is a process. When there are communication errors, the process breaks down. It is like driving a car. When a wheel falls off or the brakes don't work or the engine breaks down, the car is unable to take us to our desired destination. We automatically stop and repair the car. It is the same with communication. We cannot continue to communicate with a process that is broken down and expect good results. We have to stop and reflect on what needs to be repaired. Did we start attacking each other? Is someone shutting down? Is someone becoming angry? Is our partner not listening? These errors have to be corrected before resuming the conversation or our communication will not be productive.

Reflecting:

What is the most difficult part of being assertive?

My current challenge:

Power struggles in relationships

Power struggles occur when there is an unwillingness to negotiate and compromise due to someone's strong desire *to win*. Many power struggles escalate into a shouting match, and the only outcomes are anger and emotional exhaustion. If anyone has been drinking or using drugs, there is no point in engaging in communication because it is likely to end up in a power struggle.

If a power struggle is diagrammed, it is a pattern of one person taking a one-up position and the other person responding with another one-up statement. This pattern continues as a series of one-upping the other person. Voices escalate and body language becomes more intense. The desire to win brings forth many controlling tactics, such as accusations, blaming, and using words such as "always," "never," or "should." Statements are made such as, "You always think I am the worst person on earth!" Or, "You never care about what I want!" Or, "You should know why I'm upset if you really loved me!" Most sentences are started with "You" and are usually blame statements. In a heated argument or power struggle, the rules of respectful conflict resolution are broken, and the real issue gets lost in a flurry of anger. If the power struggle becomes too heated, the argument can escalate into physical aggression, or in contrast, one of the participants may cave in and concede because of frustration or exhaustion. In most power struggles, there are a lot of personal attacks, which feel like arrows coming from someone that we care about, and nothing is truly resolved.

Many arguments that escalate into power struggles happen over things of little importance. A good strategy is to decide what is worth an argument or what does not merit a hassle or power struggle. Often, we let ourselves start or engage in a power struggle over minor things, and in a couple of days we cannot remember what the argument was about. The stress and anger that are generated are almost always disproportionate to the problem. There may be some underlying relationship issues that are festering, and rather than discussing the *real* problem, partners engage in power struggles over minor issues. If an issue is important, both partners need to commit to talking about it rationally and agree to help solve the problem.

Though we may resolve to avoid power struggles, we may find ourselves right in the middle of an argument that is on a crash course. At this point, we need to keep in mind that in the early stages of an argument or power struggle, we can either escalate or de-escalate the argument, which requires self-control.

Power-struggle tips

- If a person tries to hook you into an argument, try to stay calm and ignore the hook. If you become drawn in, the other person is in control.
- You can refuse to engage in a power struggle in front of

children or the first thing in the morning before everyone goes to work or school. You don't want your children to start their school day being upset, and you don't want negative feelings to bleed into your whole day.
- You can stay calm and de-escalate rather than escalate the power struggle in early stages.
- Your heightened emotions can take over your rational mind. If this happens, it is important to remind yourself that if you can't speak in normal and respectful voice tones, you need to wait with the discussion until you are calmed down. Laurence Peter, a prominent educator writes: *Speak when you are angry—and you will make the best speech you'll ever regret.*
- Validating the thoughts and feelings of the other person is a way to diffuse defensiveness and anger. "That is a good idea," or, "I think I understand you, so now we need to think of how we can resolve our differences." Validating others reduces tension and defensiveness, and increases the chances for arriving at mutually agreeable solutions.
- If verbal statements become more aggressive, the best strategy is to take a break: "Let's take a time-out and have this discussion after we have both cooled down. How about 7:00 tonight?"

Power struggles simply drain personal energy, create stress and negative feelings, and nothing gets resolved. Besides having an emotional hangover, there is usually a period of silence between partners who are each stuck in negative feelings that can last for long periods of time. This is not a good use of personal energies and is not respectful of yourself or of the person you love.

◄ Anger and Guilt

> Reflecting:
>
> How can I reduce the number of power struggles?
>
> How is our relationship affected when we argue?
>
> My current challenge:

When we are in a significant relationship, we may need to remind ourselves that:

- ❖ We have no right to control others.
- ❖ Compromise is not defeat.
- ❖ Other people have a right to disagree.
- ❖ People may not love, care, and support us in ways we would like them to.

We do not have to address every irritation that happens. Letting some things go can be mature behavior, because we have learned to choose our battles. But it is a mistake to stay silent if the behavior is abusive and the emotional cost is feeling bitter and resentful. We injure ourselves when we fail to take a stand on issues that are important and emotionally abusive.

We can't change reality, but we can change the way we let frustrating events and situations affect us. Healthy anger management requires focusing on ourselves, what we are feeling, and what choices we are going to make in expressing our anger. If we emotionally step back and think seriously about the situation, we are more likely to be assertive, which requires respecting ourselves and others. If we want to be taken seriously, we need to be *reasonable and credible* when expressing our anger.

Strategies for expressing anger in relationships

- Deal with relationship issues as they arise, when they are still manageable.
- When you are angry, step back emotionally, slow down, and calmly assess the situation.
- Determine if the anger is legitimate anger or if there are errors in the way you are thinking.

Questions:

- ➢ What is the real issue?
- ➢ Is the anger coming from fear?
- ➢ Is the anger from trying to control or being controlled?
- ➢ What choices do I have regarding how I am going to express my anger?
- ➢ Should I share my feelings with a trusted friend and get a reality check before I address this situation?
- ➢ Are my angry and sarcastic expressions working for me?
- ➢ Are my expectations on others reasonable?
- ➢ Am I angry because I am not being heard or taken seriously?
- ➢ Do I need to set limits on the expectations or requests being made of me by others so that I can avoid the feelings of being overwhelmed, over-extended and as a result, prone to angry outbursts?
- ➢ What can I dismiss, let go of, and quit fighting about?

◄ Anger and Guilt

- If your reaction is disproportionate to the irritation, there are likely to be internal anger issues that are brewing within you that need to be addressed. By working with your past anger, you can prevent future flashes of anger, which are disrespectful and frightening to others.
- Avoid confronting when feelings are intense. Breathing deeply helps to calm down and gain self-control. If necessary, take a time-out and do a physical activity like walking, cleaning, or reaching out and doing something to help others.
- When you are ready to address the anger situation, schedule time for working things out. It is helpful for everyone to agree to certain rules:
  - ✓ Agree to no name-calling or profanity
  - ✓ Agree to tell the truth
  - ✓ Agree to try to solve the problem
  - ✓ Agree to refrain from controlling, manipulating, interrupting, blaming, shaming, and ridiculing

- Use calming self-talk to gain your composure:
  - ➢ I will remain calm.
  - ➢ I have choices regarding how I am going to react.
  - ➢ This situation is stirring up old anger and I need to separate my past anger from this current situation.
  - ➢ I can asked to be heard if I am being ignored.
  - ➢ I deserve to be taken seriously.
  - ➢ I have self-control and can choose my responses.
  - ➢ I do not have to respond immediately.
  - ➢ I can confront dishonesty.
  - ➢ I can ask questions if I need more specifics.
  - ➢ I will not interrupt the other person.
  - ➢ I will not become defensive.
  - ➢ I can excuse myself and walk away.

> I will listen intently.
> I will be honest with my feelings if I feel emotionally safe.
> I can decide if I have the problem or if I am being blamed for the problem.
> I will respect this person's viewpoint, even though I may disagree.
> I can choose whether I will internalize this anger or let it go.
> I am committed to work toward a positive resolution.
> I have personal power and use it wisely, honestly, and with caring.
> I will express my thoughts and feelings using normal voice tones.
> I am confident and competent.
> I deserve respect and to be taken seriously if I am respectful.
> I will speak in ways that maintain my credibility.
> I am remaining calm.

- Acknowledge that people are different. There are many ways of viewing the same situation. Different perspectives and ways of reacting do not necessarily mean that one person is right and the other person is wrong. If you are fighting to win or be right, it will create more distance in your relationship. If you are seeking to understand the other person and are willing to negotiate, there is likely to be a resolution that will create emotional closeness, rather than distance.
- Listen attentively. Wait your turn to speak. Clarify what you are hearing by repeating back to the other person what you heard them say.
- Identify the current problem. Don't drag up old grudges or

make a marathon out of the conversation. If you are responsible for the problem, take ownership. Amends may be in order.
- Speak in normal voice tones. State feelings directly, honestly, and respectfully. Avoid blaming others for the difficulty or for the way you feel. Using words such as "never" and "always" are sure ways to intensify the anger. It's more effective to say, "I have noticed that this happens *often*." Use "I" messages, saying, "I think…, I feel…, I fear…, I want…"
- Generate win-win rather than win-lose situations. Strive for resolutions that are mutually beneficial.
- Be affirming when there is successful resolution of problems.

When you speak or confront in a confident manner, you establish a presence that is more apt to be respected and taken seriously. You can then state your boundaries. A constructive use of anger helps you to "draw a line in the sand" as to what you will not tolerate, but you also need to have a plan of action if your line in the sand is ignored, stepped on, or ridiculed.

When you are aware that you have choices as to how to handle angry feelings, you are more able to bring the anger under control and decrease its intensity. If you have anger skills, you will feel more in control of yourself, less threatened, and less defensive. You are taking charge of yourself rather than letting someone have power over you, which is being proactive rather than reactive.

When your relationship is dysfunctional, despite your best efforts to communicate assertively, you may feel that you have no options. However, there are options, all of which pose their own difficulties. You can: 1) Stay angry, which is not healthy for you; 2) Modify the time spent in the relationship; 3) Emotionally detach from the relationship and learn to take better care of yourself or: 4) Leave a relationship if it continues to be toxic and children are being harmed emotionally, mentally, or physically.

Reasons for anger may change as you evolve

Winston Churchill said, "A man is about as big as the things that make him angry." As you emotionally mature, the reasons for your anger will often change. You will be less apt to be angry at minor irritations. Road-rage is often demonstrated by people who have many other anger issues. As you evolve, rather than being angry at a careless driver, you may be grateful that you were not harmed and acknowledge that you have probably made the same driving mistake. You no longer get angry at people who take too long in the grocery line, and you probably find ways to pass the few minutes of time. Maturity results in experiencing anger over larger problems, such as child abuse and neglect, social injustices, or racial and religious prejudice. As you evolve, you are likely to become more willing to invest your anger energies in working to create positive changes, such as speaking out against oppression, pornography, and violent media productions.

Strategies for dealing with anger directed toward you

When others direct anger at you, it's important to sort out the communication to objectively determine what to acknowledge as your responsibility and what to reject as anger being misdirected at you. The anger may come from legitimate concerns or grievances. You might have done or said something offensive, failed to be responsible, or made an error that adversely affected the other person. Or, the anger might not belong to you. For example, if your partner arrives home frustrated and goes on an angry tirade about things that happened at work, the anger is being projected on you, but you have nothing to do with the anger. However, you are probably willing to

◄ Anger and Guilt

listen to the anger if it is prefaced by an explanation, such as, "I had a bad day and just need to vent. Are you willing to listen to me?"

Here are some suggestions to take care of yourself when aggressive anger is directed toward you:

1. Make sure you are safe if the person is likely to become physically aggressive with his/her anger. Call police if necessary.
2. Having other people around will often diffuse the situation and decrease abusive anger statements.
3. Assess the situation. If a person is intoxicated, excuse yourself and set another time for discussion.
4. Give the angry person space and make sure there is a way for you to leave the room.
5. Do not try to correct information when someone is being verbally aggressive and there's a possibility of physical violence.
6. Avoid scolding and shaming, which is likely to intensify the person's anger.
7. Encourage the angry person to sit down. The likelihood of anger turning into violence decreases when people are sitting down.
8. Listen and do not become defensive. If it is safe to question the other person, ask for specific details when there are accusing generalizations such as "You always make me so angry." You might say, "I would like to understand your feelings more clearly. Can you give me an example?"
9. Try to stay calm.
10. Agree to valid points and make a choice to ignore or confront wrong information after the person has settled down.
11. If actual errors were made by you that triggered the other person's anger, apologies need to be offered, along with describing how the problem will be corrected.

- Rhonda shares:

    I work in customer service and seldom get complaints, but when I do, it can be a frightening and exhausting experience. I have learned not to get defensive, even if the information they are spewing out is totally false. I just let them vent and eventually they start calming down. When they are calm, I clarify any information that was not factual in a diplomatic way and focus on what needs to be done to solve the problem. Sometimes I ask them what they need and then I'll see if I can arrange to have that need met. This works because they feel heard. I have the advantage of working behind a counter, and there are others around me, so safety is usually not an issue. But it takes awhile to emotionally recover after I have been a target of someone's anger.

How do I currently deal with anger directed toward me?

Anger strategies that I can use when someone is angry with me:

Anger generated by irrational thoughts and beliefs

We may be creating anger within ourselves because of *irrational thoughts and beliefs such as:*

- ✓ I should be able to change the behaviors of another person, and I get angry when they don't change.

Anger and Guilt

- ✓ People should respond to my requests immediately, and if they don't, I have a right to be angry.
- ✓ I want to be the center of attention, and when I am not, I get angry.
- ✓ The worst things always happen to me, and I'm angry a lot of the time.
- ✓ People are out to get whatever they can from me. I always end up being taken advantage of and I get angry.
- ✓ I'm angry inside but never let it out because I don't want to look bad.
- ✓ People should think like I think, and when they don't, I get angry.
- ✓ When I fail in one area of my life, I am a total failure and I get angry at myself.
- ✓ Other people *make* my life miserable and I get angry.
- ✓ It's not my fault and I can't help it if I get angry.
- ✓ I am helpless, weak, inadequate, vulnerable, powerless, and angry.

- John shares:

    I was convinced that people were out to make my life miserable. I was often angry because people were so stupid. I'd wake up in the morning and wonder who was going to screw me over today. I didn't understand people who were always so calm. I decided it was because they just didn't care. I think girlfriends broke up with me because of my anger, but they never told me why they left. I don't have a clue how to get rid of my anger. The anger I feel has always been with me, and it doesn't take much to set me off.

Changing our irrational thinking reduces anger

We can acknowledge angry feelings and trace them back to angry thoughts, which may be legitimate or may be untrue, distorted, or exaggerated. Continuing to have the same irrational or negative thoughts and beliefs will result in continuing to generate toxic anger.

Thoughts and beliefs create our perceptions and feelings, including anger. Changing our irrational thoughts and beliefs involves the following process:

1. Identify the angry thought or belief.
2. Challenge the angry thought or belief:
   - ✓ Is there any basis in reality to support this thought or belief as being true?
   - ✓ Does this thought or belief have words such as "never" or "always"? If so, it probably is irrational, exaggerated, or false.
   - ✓ Is this thought or belief life-fostering or life-diminishing?
   - ✓ Is this thought or belief fear-based?
3. If the thought or belief is determined to be irrational and life-diminishing, dismiss the thought.
4. Create a realistic thought or belief to replace the irrational thought or belief.
5. Continue life with the new thought or belief. When other irrational thoughts or beliefs occur, use this same process. If you are diligent in refining your thoughts and beliefs, you will discover that the frequency of your irrational thoughts or beliefs decreases, which means you are creating less anger for yourself.

◄ Anger and Guilt

For example:

1. Identify the irrational thought or belief: *People always take advantage of me and I get angry.*
2. Challenge the thought: *Do people take advantage of me or do I let people take advantage of me? Can other people make me feel angry? Or, is anger a choice I am making?*
3. If the thought or belief is determined to be irrational and life-diminishing, revise the thought or belief: *It feels like people take advantage of me, but maybe it's because I don't stand up for myself. It feels like others* make *me feel angry, but no one can* make *me feel angry.*
4. Create a realistic thought or belief to replace the irrational thought or belief: *I can set limits with people.*
5. Continue life with the new thought or belief: *I am setting limits and when I need to, I can say, 'No.' If I choose to be angry, I can express my anger appropriately.*
6. Correct future irrational thoughts and beliefs.

We may not be able to eliminate all situations that cause us to be angry, but thinking more clearly and rationally can result in a major reduction in the amount of anger we experience. Common sense tells us that there are enough situations in life that cause us to be angry, so we don't want to be generating more anger for ourselves by our irrational thinking and beliefs.

Helping children with their anger

We often fail to directly teach children how to deal with difficult emotions, especially anger. However, they watch and learn from adults. As a result, the behaviors that children experience from their parents are likely to be the same behaviors that parents will, at some point, experience from their children, whether they are positive or negative. With a growing awareness about the feeling of anger and how to deal with it effectively, many parents are modeling and teaching their children how to express their anger in healthy ways.

Reasons for children's' anger

- ✓ Physical, sexual, emotional, and verbal abuse or neglect
- ✓ Mental or behavioral disabilities
- ✓ Excessive parental control
- ✓ Unmet emotional, psychological, educational, social, and/or physical needs
- ✓ Unmet developmental needs:
  - To belong
  - To be me
  - To be someone
  - To go beyond, which involves continued learning and expanding
- ✓ Adjustments that they are expected to make based on parents' choices, such as divorce
- ✓ Having chaotic schedules and environments
- ✓ Having to adjust to a parent's new relationship or a step-family
- ✓ Being hungry, lonely, tired, feeling unloved or that there is no one to trust
- ✓ Modeling parents' aggressive anger but being told they shouldn't be angry
- ✓ Feeling that they have no rights or choices and, therefore, feel powerless
- ✓ Watching violence on television or playing violent video games

◄ Anger and Guilt

As a parent, there may have been times when you struggled with your children's anger. The first step is to learn about the feeling of anger and develop strategies to deal with your own anger more effectively. In families, as with all organizations, a good principle is: "a rule for one is a rule for all." This requires *all* family members to express anger in appropriate ways. Inappropriate and unacceptable expressions of anger for both parents and children are kicking, hitting, yelling, screaming, having temper tantrums, blaming others, or physically harming family members or pets. The more skills you have regarding anger, the easier your parenting experience will be and the less stress your children will experience. Problems and challenging situations are discussed in respectful ways and in normal voice tones. You will not always handle your anger well as a parent. After angry words or outbursts, it's important to apologize for your inappropriate, aggressive anger expressions. You are a powerful model to your children, and they learn many behaviors directly from you.

Teaching anger skills to children will help them throughout their life. Children naturally experience angry feelings like adults and are never at fault for feeling their emotions. Children may not have words for their anger, so they frequently act out their anger aggressively toward others or toward objects. Encourage children to express their anger in ways that are not harmful to themselves or others. When your children are angry, take some time to discuss the problem that has created the anger. If young children have not developed language to express feelings, it may be helpful to have them draw a picture of how they feel and ask them to talk about their picture.

If your children are old enough and have language skills, encourage them to "use your words" and talk about the feelings. Teach your children to relax and calm down by breathing deeply when they are angry. When children are expressing anger, the facts may not always be right because of their interpretation of a situation. Let them keep talking and, after the anger has been expressed, correct any inaccurate information, if necessary. Use the anger situation as a teachable moment, and take the time to talk about how to express anger in healthy ways. If you can find out what a child's anger is about, there may be a relatively easy solution. In other situations that cannot be changed, try to help him/her to deal with it in healthy ways.

To reduce the number of power struggles with children, offer them choices. There are many areas in family life that are negotiable. Children feel like they have some personal power when given choices, and will more readily accept the non-negotiable, fair, and reasonable family rules that are necessary to coexist cooperatively. You may have to wait for the child to think about the choices, or they will feel like it is an ultimatum and rebellious behaviors may increase.

Sometimes our adult decisions make children angry. If children become angry, for example, for having to stop an activity that may not be safe, we can talk to the child, telling the child that it is okay to feel angry, but then explaining what was necessary. For example, "It's okay to be angry with me, but I had to tell you to stop unbuckling your seat belt because you wouldn't be safe."

Other suggestions for dealing with children's anger:

- ✓ Set limits. Do not accept aggressive anger outbursts from your children or adults in the home.
- ✓ Involve the child in family meetings, where good things are shared as well as family problems. Invite the child to share in the rule-making and the consequences.
- ✓ Speak directly to the child about inappropriate anger expressions as soon as it is possible to have private time. Invite the

◄ Anger and Guilt

- child to talk about his/her anger.
- ✓ If you are in a private place, offer a towel to twist or a pillow to punch and teach the child to release anger by being physical in ways that are not harmful.
- ✓ If the anger is escalating, offer choices: "Can you get yourself under control or do you choose to take a time-out to calm down?" As the parent, you may want to say, "Sometimes I take a time-out when I am upset. It helps me to calm down so I can make good choices and act better."
- ✓ When children are able to understand, teach the relationship between behaviors and consequences. Explaining natural consequences is different from making threats about what will happen.
- ✓ Talk about the angry behaviors rather than verbally attacking or shaming the child, which causes the child to feel inadequate or unloved.
- ✓ Do not allow the viewing of violence on television or playing violent video games.

Key Points:

1. Reasons for being angry include painful childhood experiences, significant losses in our life, anger experienced in our relationships, and anger generated by our irrational thoughts and beliefs.
2. The grieving process is emotionally healing and involves the stages of denial, anger, bargaining, depression, and acceptance.
3. The anger that is generated within relationships is often about power, money, sex, division of household and financial responsibilities, parenting, infidelity, and in-laws.
4. Children have legitimate reasons to be angry, including

when they are physically, sexually, mentally, or emotionally abused or when their basic needs are not met.
5. In families, a good principle to follow is that a rule for one is a rule for all. All family members need to express anger appropriately.
6. Refuse to allow the viewing of violence on television or video games.
7. Our responsibility as adults is to model healthy, nonviolent, and appropriate anger expressions to our children.

Chapter 4

Strategies for Working with Anger

Anger can be a pervasive and intense feeling that often overshadows other feelings. Angry feelings are like young children who pester parents until they are acknowledged, but when given attention, they will stop their pleading and move on to other activities. When we listen to our feelings, they become less intrusive and powerful because they have been acknowledged and their messages have been received. If we do not listen and learn from our angry feelings, we are likely to accumulate a considerable amount of anger, which adversely affects our emotional life and spills into our relationships. If we are carrying anger from the past, we may hesitate, be fearful, and cringe at the suggestion to go inward and work with our anger. We wonder if we will lose control or if our anger will consume us. The reality is that we are more likely to lose control if we continue to suppress our anger, which can fester and build into an internal volcano.

When we fail to develop the skills involved in dealing with anger, the mental, physical, emotional, and spiritual dimensions of our life experience are adversely affected. If we carry high levels of anger within, we need to connect with the ***real*** causes of our anger and address the past hurts, rather than suppressing them or projecting our anger on others. When we decide to do anger work, we are deciding to work on ourselves. We acknowledge that we are harboring

Anger and Guilt

personal anger that needs our attention. We can work with our anger in privacy, in ways that do not harm ourselves or others, knowing that when we are carrying internal anger, we are less able to be a healthy partner or parent. Learning how to deal with our anger in healthy ways will enhance our overall life experience.

Having words for our angry feelings

Often, it is difficult for us to find the right words to describe what triggers our anger. When we discover a word to describe the feeling, we can then "pin it down" and make it real to us. The following are examples of words that might be difficult to describe, regarding our feelings or experiences:

- I am angry because I feel that I am being *controlled*.
- I'm not getting what I want and I'm angry.
- I am provoked and am starting to feel angry.
- I am feeling impatient, irritable, and angry.
- I am angry because I was confronted about my behaviors.
- I am angry because I feel like I am being held hostage in my relationship.
- I feel pressured and manipulated and am becoming angry.
- I am angry because my beliefs are being challenged.

Naming the feeling clarifies it. When we *name* the feeling, we can then work with the feeling. It is ours. We have more choices as to what we are going to do with the feeling. We may say, "Oh, that's why I am angry! Now I understand where my anger is coming from." When we give ourselves permission to be angry, we can start healing by releasing our anger in healthy ways, rather than suppressing and avoiding the anger within ourselves.

Years ago, I took a Dale Carnegie class, and one of the

assignments for the upcoming week was to think of something that was angry-making in our lives. The directions were to bring a newspaper to the next class, prepared to express our anger-making issue to a Dale Carnegie classmate. The instructions were to talk, yell, or scream out our anger while pounding the newspaper on a table. We were not supposed to stop until our partner decided we had fully and sincerely expressed and released our anger. When we had completed our anger work, we exchanged roles with our partner. Since there were twenty people doing this exercise at the same time, we didn't have to worry about looking foolish or out of control, because everyone was doing anger-releasing work.

This experience was the first time anyone had given me permission and encouraged me to acknowledge and express anger. After releasing the anger, the anger issue seemed to fade away. When the course was completed, we were asked to write about the most beneficial session in the fourteen weeks of class. I was not alone in choosing this exercise, which was Session Five. As we processed the experience, many people shared that they felt better because they had released the anger that they had been carrying within themselves for a long time.

Anger is emotional energy

Anger is emotional energy. Our anger energy can be suppressed and fester into resentments, hatred, or depression. It is energy-consuming just to keep our suppressed anger contained within ourselves. When we try to hold in our anger, we tighten up and store the anger in our muscles and/or in our jaw. We may experience physical problems such as aching muscles, headaches, backaches, joint pain, and constipation. Anger energy can also escalate into a full-blown rage that is harmful to ourselves and others.

Our mind-body-spirit healing will involve releasing our anger energy in safe ways. By working through our anger, or using our anger for motivation for creative and positive action, our energy flows easily and smoothly, and we are more able to evolve to higher levels of emotional and physical well-being. We may wonder if releasing our anger is releasing negativity into the universe, which we may think is contrary to spiritual principles. But we can speculate that God wants us to be emotionally healthy and knows that working through our anger is part of our healing process. Releasing the anger energy by ourselves in privacy or sharing our anger assertively in efforts to solve problems is far less harmful than lashing out at others and emotionally and physically harming them.

Anger prevention and intervention

Working with our anger is a process that needs to start with ***prevention***. By being proactive, we can prevent many situations that cause anger by changing our thoughts and behaviors. However, it's not possible to prevent all situations that cause anger. When we feel angry, we can then do an ***intervention*** on ourselves. When we successfully implement both prevention and intervention, we will experience less anger within ourselves, and our anger outbursts will be rare.

Prevention Strategies

Realize that anger is a feeling and feelings are neither good nor evil.
Be knowledgeable about anger and take responsibility for how your anger is expressed. If it is suppressed, you are harming yourself. If anger is expressed aggressively, it is abusive to others and destroys relationships.

Be aware of irrational thoughts and beliefs that create unnecessary anger. Become more self-disciplined and positive with your thinking.
Deal with problems when they are still manageable, rather than letting them accumulate, which increases the chances of having a blowup or meltdown.
Work through past anger so it doesn't infuse angry emotions into current situations.
Learn to be assertive, rather than passive, passive-aggressive, or aggressive when expressing your anger.
Prevent anger by giving up the need to control others.
Prevent anger by giving up the need to be the center of attention.
Prevent anger by reducing the amount of time spent with toxic persons.
Eliminate viewing television violence or playing violent video games.
Learn to set limits to prevent overextension, which is an effective way to take better care of yourself.
Be proactive and decide what situations need to be addressed, and what situations can be dismissed as unimportant.
Release your personal anger in safe ways, which helps you to be more rational when you are experiencing challenging situations in relationships.
Never make problems larger than they need to be.
Don't expect other people, especially children, to have the same time-table or priorities as you do.
Have correct information and be sure to understand the background and context of a situation before becoming angry about an issue.
Make sure that expectations of others are reasonable.

◄ Anger and Guilt

If sarcasm underlies a person's statement, ignore or confront the sarcasm.
Ignore minor irritations.
Remind yourself that: ❖ You have no right to control others. ❖ Compromise is not defeat. ❖ Other people have a right to disagree. ❖ People may not love, care about, and support you in ways you would like them to.
Refuse to internalize destructive criticism and view it as truth.
Change negative attitudes into positive attitudes.

Anger Intervention Strategies

Stop, think, and make a conscious choice whether a situation needs to be addressed or whether it can be dismissed. Take a time-out and breathe deeply. If the anger is too intense, take time to walk, exercise, or talk with a trusted friend before expressing the anger to the person involved.
Use calming and rational self-talk so that you can think more clearly about what action is most appropriate to the situation.
Be assertive, which is being honest, open, and respectful of others.
Express anger only when you are calm enough to communicate effectively and appropriately.
Recognize the anger that is generated by irrational thoughts and make the necessary and positive changes in the way you are thinking.
Set personal limits when necessary and say "no" in appropriate ways.

Self-challenge with "Am I making this a bigger deal than it needs to be?"
View the problem objectively and approach it rationally, step by step.
Change negative attitudes into positive attitudes.

The importance of deep breathing

When we are angry, scared, frightened, or stressed, we often forget to breathe deeply. Deep breathing helps us when we are experiencing the many different forms of stress, nourishes every cell of our body, and promotes relaxation. Endorphins, which are the body's natural painkillers, are released to relieve headaches, sleeplessness, backaches, and other stress-related pain. When we feel anger rising within ourselves, breathing deeply will help us remain calm and in control of our anger. Taking the time to breathe will also give us a few moments to decide how we are going to respond to a situation that is creating anger.

Besides being proactive and preventing anger, as well as intervening on ourselves when we are angry, there are several other strategies we can use when dealing with our anger. ***The rule of anger work is to not harm ourselves or others,*** and all of these anger strategies follow that rule.

Anger Strategy 1: Increase your self-awareness by writing in a journal

Journaling is a good way to develop self-awareness. By writing down your thoughts and feelings, you can explore the causes for your anger. Your anger may be legitimate and valid because you have experienced harm or injustice. Or, your anger could be anger

◂ Anger and Guilt

that you are carrying from past emotional hurts, including childhood abuse or traumatic losses, which may be the most intense kind of anger that people experience. If you have unrealistic expectations of others that they do not meet, you may become angry. You may be generating anger because of irrational thinking and beliefs. You may have anger at yourself for your own unacceptable behaviors; or anger that you are creating because your attempts to control others are not being successful. You may also feel angry because you cannot escape from a toxic relationship.

Find a comfortable and quiet place to journal. Before writing, breathe deeply several times to relax. You may want to make sure your journal is kept in a private and secure place so that you know that no one else will be reading it. When you journal, you don't have to censor your words. There is no right way or wrong way to write in your journal. You don't have to be reasonable, nice, have neat handwriting, or have correct grammar. You can be completely honest in your private journal. No one is going to read your journal and make judgments on you, so you don't have to be guarded. Your writing may turn into angry scribbling, pictures, or diagrams. You can be in the moment and let go of your anger and other feelings, rather than suppressing, minimizing, or denying your anger. Putting your emotions into words clarifies your feelings and decreases the intensity of the anger and other troublesome feelings. When you are journaling your anger, you will be able to view it as being momentarily external to yourself, which provides some objectivity. You may want to save your journal writings to read at a later time in your life. I remember reading some of my own anger journals. After reading a few entries, I set the journal aside and thought, "I'm glad the anger is on paper and not in my body or I would be very ill, either emotionally or physically."

Your anger may be involved with painful experiences in your childhood, although you may not have clear memories of what

Strategies for Working with Anger

happened. However, if you give yourself mental permission, and are open to reviewing them, these memories will come forward in your mind. As you recall the painful experiences, write down the memories, the feelings and the anger and sadness involved.

If you have a difficult time getting started writing in your journal, some prompters may be helpful:

- The real reason I am angry is:
- The person that I am really angry at is…
- I am angry at what happened in my childhood:
- What I learned about anger from my father was…
- When my mother was angry, she…

When you are experiencing *current* situations that are creating frustration and anger, journaling will help you to settle down, gain clarity on the situation, and view the options. If you plan to confront, you can plan a confrontation that is direct, honest, and respectful.

Collecting data about your current anger can be done by recalling your last anger situation and how you responded. You can evaluate how you expressed your anger, either positively or negatively. If your response was inappropriate, ineffective, or harmful to self or others, it will be helpful to journal about what you can do better the next time you are angry.

- Becky shares:

    I never thought about writing out my anger because I thought I was not supposed to be angry! But when I started writing, three things happened that I didn't expect. First, I was surprised at how much anger just kept coming out on the page! My writing became increasingly wild and crazy. My second experience was how much more calm I was after

Anger and Guilt

my journaling sessions. Sometimes I felt almost empty. But the emptiness felt good. Last, I came to understand my anger better. Some of my current anger is when my spouse doesn't pitch in and help. I become angry, but say nothing because I don't want a long, drawn-out argument. I feel that I am doing most of the work, both outside and inside the home, and increasingly, I am angry, but so far, I haven't said anything.

Anger Strategy 2: Respond to the anger you have with yourself

Anger stands ready to provide the motivation to start what we need to start, finish what we need to finish, stop what we need to stop, release what we need to release, confront what we need to confront, clean what we need to clean, repair what we need to repair, and move ourselves out of "park" and go forward with our life that we, alone, design. To review, our anger can provide the motivation to change behaviors when we are angry at ourselves for:

- Eating too much
- Not exercising
- Being lazy
- Spending too much money
- Drinking too much alcohol and having another miserable hangover
- Getting a DUI or speeding ticket
- Smoking
- Receiving late fees and/or overdraft charges
- Wasting time
- Caving in to the manipulations of controllers
- Facing consequences that we could have prevented if we were responsible
- Agreeing to do things we don't want to do

- Not entering treatment for an addiction
- Not making difficult decisions about our life and moving forward toward our goals

In these and other types of situations, we can listen to anger as a friend, hear the message and act on it, rather than continually reprimanding ourselves for not taking action. When we listen to our anger regarding these types of behaviors, it is usually obvious what we need to do. If there is a reason that we are unable to act on what our anger is communicating to us, we can access help, such as therapy or a recovery program, a life coach, or support for anxiety or depression.

Anger Strategy 3: Stand firm in a neutral position

We can observe the way controllers act in the one-up and one-down power positions. Controllers often use anger to put us in a one-down position so that we will comply. Just because someone tries to put us in a one-down, inferior position doesn't mean we have to go there, unless there is a safety concern. Controllers aren't sure what to do when someone stands firm in an assertive, equal, neutral position, which is neither one-up and superior, nor one-down and inferior. Often, if we maintain our credibility and understand the one-up, one-down dynamic, we can experience much more success in being heard. We can make a statement that is in a neutral power position, neither one-up or one-down, and repeat the statement if necessary. This is a way of assertively self-advocating, rather than caving in to the manipulations of controlling people.

Anger Strategy 4: Exercise in non-competitive ways

Body movement is helpful to release angry feelings. Taking a brisk walk, jogging, or working out by hitting balls in a racquetball court, punching a punching bag, lifting weights, twisting a towel, or hitting pillows are good ways to release anger. Some people use a small, flat drum and drum out percussion patterns to release their anger. Besides being an outlet for the anger, physical activity produces endorphins that will help you feel better. If the exercise is routine and you don't have to actively engage your mind, you can visualize the anger being released from your body as you exercise.

Anger Strategy 5: Do anger work outdoors in nature

Processing and releasing your anger can be done while doing outdoor activities such as cleaning up branches, planting trees, or working in a garden. Anger can be released by chopping wood, throwing stones into a body of water, hiking or biking on the nature trails. Use your mind to imagine the anger saying good-bye and leaving your mind and body.

Anger Strategy 6: Express your anger through movement

When you harbor anger, your physical body is involved as well as your mind. You may be able to release your anger by using your mind, but combining thoughts with body movement is even more effective. Verbalize your anger and use your body to act out and possibly exaggerate your emotions, including your anger. Holler and scream if it feels helpful and if you have privacy. Allow yourself to feel your feelings. Put actions to your feelings. Create and act out a serious or a humorous performance to release your anger and stress. There is a powerful scene in the movie "...And Justice for All" (Columbia Pictures, 1979) regarding anger. An attorney who was angry at the injustice and ineffectiveness of the legal system hurtles plates down the hall of the courthouse building. You may relate to that scene and wish you had the opportunity to throw dishes and hear the glass breaking.

- Macy shares:

    I discovered that I release my anger much better if I use my body to express my anger. I can't just keep thinking about my anger because then it just gets worse. A few weeks ago I planned a weekend by myself at the lake and promised myself to work through my anger from being physically abused when I was a child. I brought large pieces of paper, markers, and some marching music. I started drawing out my anger and then I decided to act out my anger. As I was kicking and making punching gestures with my arms, it started to thunder and lightning. That was the perfect background for my anger-releasing! I took that as a sign from God, who was helping me to heal from the anger that I had been carrying since my childhood. And when I drove home after that weekend, I felt like a new person, and that feeling has continued.

Anger Strategy 7: Talk out your anger with a person that you trust

Talking with a trusted friend who understands how important it is to express all feelings, including anger, can be very helpful. However, you don't want to overload your friends by having the same conversation repeatedly. There are interactions that relieve stress and others that create a higher level of stress. You may decide to seek out an anger class or support group if your anger is intense, pervasive, and routinely creating problems for you.

Anger Strategy 8: Self-advocate by confronting

When you are experiencing unfairness and control in a relationship, it's important to speak up, even though it may be easier to remain quiet. Making attempts to change unhealthy relationship dynamics is important to prevent future hurts, misunderstandings, and conflict. First, you have to calm down if you are highly agitated so that you are credible when confronting abusive behaviors. It's important to speak with a calm voice and be specific.

With past anger, it may be helpful to write a letter to the person involved. In the first draft, let go, do not censor your words, and write everything you want to say but probably wouldn't say if you were face-to-face with the person. After you have released your anger in the first draft letter, you can revise your writing until you are expressing exactly what you want to say. If you decide to send the letter, it is best to edit your writing so that the letter does not have so much anger that you lose credibility. Sharing your feelings in a respectful, honest way maintains your dignity, and you are more likely to be acknowledged and taken seriously.

Anger Strategy 9: Be productive with your anger

Invest the anger energy into doing various jobs such as yard work, cleaning, shoveling snow, washing a vehicle, or other physical tasks. These activities can also be a time-out period to provide some relief from the intense anger feelings and give you time to sort through your feelings, gain perspective, and make healthy choices about what you need to do.

Anger Strategy 10: Use self-calming strategies

Breathing deeply is the best way to relax your body. When we feel anger rising within ourselves, breathing deeply will help us remain calm and in control of our anger. Taking the time to breathe will also give us a few moments to decide how we are going to respond to a situation that is creating anger. When breathing, visualize your anger leaving your body, both the anger you know about and the anger that you are possibly carrying that is not in your awareness. As you breathe, imagine the anger leaving and being replaced by positive energy flowing into your mind and body.

Anger Strategy 11: Join a support group, such as a Twelve-Step program

Twelve-Step recovery groups change people's lives, not only because the members have sobriety, but the program offers a spiritual way to live, an emotionally safe place to express feelings, and a sponsor to support you as you learn and grow. In Twelve-Step groups, people express their anger and other feelings openly and honestly. Participating in these groups may be your first experience with people sharing their feelings so readily. Recovery and other types of support groups are safe places to express your anger or other feelings because you will not be judged, criticized, or shamed. Healing happens in support groups, as evidenced by members' positive changes in behaviors, which leads to living a more productive and fulfilling life.

Anger Strategy 12: Use music to help process your anger

Listening or playing music that is bold and powerful will help you get in touch with your anger. Sing along with music that has lyrics that help you to identify and describe your experiences and feelings. Some parts of classical music, marching music, or some of the current popular music can be helpful to express and release your anger in effective and non-harmful ways.

Anger Strategy 13: Attend a retreat, workshop, or healing session

There are anger retreats or group therapy opportunities where you can join with others in expressing and releasing your anger. If you travel to a different town and are with people you have never met and will never see again, you will have fewer inhibitions. When you see others working through their anger, you will be more able to give yourself permission to let go, experience your anger energies, and start expressing whatever you feel. You will often hear people sharing stories that resonate with your own life experiences. It is easier to be absolutely truthful about your anger when you hear others doing the same. As with any anger work, you have to get beyond self-directives such as, "be nice, don't share feelings, always speak with kind words, and don't ever show your anger."

Breath work therapists facilitate a breathing process that provides access to repressed emotions and painful feelings that may be stored in the physical body. Each person focuses on their internal process. Participants, whether they work individually or in a group, report that they experience healing at a very deep emotional and physical level when they do breath work therapy.

Body movement techniques, such as Tai Chi and Qigong, increase energy, which flows more freely within the body. Reiki is an energy technique which restores the flow of energy that has been disrupted or blocked by trauma, negativity, anger, or unresolved emotions.

Many of the natural ways of healing are based on ancient forms of health care. When any of these practices are chosen and integrated into your lifestyle, you will feel the positive benefits in many areas of your life.

Strategies for Working with Anger

Anger Strategy 14: Use the Serenity Prayer

You can reduce a considerable amount of your anger by daily embracing the wisdom of the Serenity Prayer: *God grant me the serenity to accept the things I cannot change, courage to change the things I can, and wisdom to know the difference.*

Anger Strategy 15: Visualize the person who has been abusive to you and talk to her/him

Face an empty chair and speak to the image in your mind of the person who harmed you or who is currently harming you. Stand up to feel more powerful as you speak to the imaginary person in the chair. Do not censor your words. Say everything that you need to say in any way that helps you to release your anger. Let all of your feelings out, without minimizing the hurt that you experienced. This is also an effective way to rehearse what you will say if you choose to actually meet and confront the person who harmed you.

Anger Strategy 16: Transform your anger energy into positive creations or actions

Transform the anger energy and create art, music, or invest your anger energy in a cause greater than yourself. Become a child advocate, join a peace rally, become a Red Cross volunteer, work for the elimination of hunger, or discover ways to support homeless people. Work for any cause you consider to be healthy and worthwhile. Mahatma Gandhi modeled how anger energy can be invested in a cause greater than oneself. When he was a young man in South Africa, he was removed from a train because he refused to surrender his first-class ticket and move to the third-class compartment. He was enraged by what had been done to him, as well as the many injustices his people suffered. Gandhi resolved to work for justice in a nonviolent way so that all people were treated fairly and respectfully. He transformed his rage and used it for motivation to work for equality, human dignity, and the value of all persons. We can do the same in our own unique ways.

Anger Strategy 17: Use mental imagery and visualize your anger leaving your body

You can use your creative mind to form mental pictures. There may be anger that you are aware of, and anger that is below your level of awareness. Visualize all of the anger as being released from your mind, emotions, and physical body. Besides anger, you can visualize other negativity leaving you. At the end of a visualization session, imagine a place that is peaceful and calming, breathe deeply, and return slowly into full awareness.

Anger Strategy 18: Use affirmations

Use affirmations that strengthen your resolutions regarding anger, such as:

- I am not willing to be controlled by someone's anger.
- I am releasing my anger from my mind and body.
- I view my anger as a friendly messenger.
- I can ask for what I need.
- Today I choose thoughts that are supportive and nourishing.
- I can express my anger assertively.
- I take good care of my mental, emotional, physical, and spiritual self.
- I am grateful for all of my blessings.
- My life keeps getting better and better.

Strategies for Working with Anger

Our anger diminishes when we are diligent in preventing anger, intervening on ourselves, working through and releasing our anger. We will feel clear and have fewer angry days. Situations that used to trigger our anger will seldom create an emotional upset. Physical symptoms are likely to decrease because we have less stress due to being angry. Our body will be more relaxed. Our communication will improve, and we will be able to address difficulties with calmness. We will experience being set free from the anger that probably began in childhood. Our minds, bodies, emotions, and spirit will rejoice in this freedom.

When we do emotional releasing of our anger, we may reach the point of feeling empty, like being in an emotional void. Our healing process often follows the pattern of moving out of denial and working through past hurtful experiences, questioning and sorting out our beliefs, and grieving our losses. Feeling an emotional void is *positive* because it indicates that emotional work has actually happened, and that there has been a mental, emotional, and spiritual clearing of repressed feelings, false notions, and life-diminishing thoughts. This empty place within can now be filled with truthful beliefs about ourselves, others, and the world, and more positive ways of thinking and behaving. We can now have access to the energies that have been previously consumed by suppressing our anger, being passive and manipulative with our anger, or expressing our anger in hurtful ways. With these new energies, we are more able to create and activate a new design for our lives. This will involve a new way of living because we have made peace with our past hurtful experiences and losses; made peace with the questions we have no answers for; and made peace with those we love, even if they pose difficulties for us at times.

◄ Anger and Guilt

> What anger strategies work for me?
>
> My current anger challenge:

Key Points:

1. The mental, physical, emotional, and spiritual dimensions of our life experience are adversely affected when we lack anger skills and express anger in ineffective ways.
2. Learning anger skills involves prevention of anger and intervention on ourselves when we are angry.
3. Anger-releasing strategies include journaling, physical exercise, or transforming the anger energy into positive action.
4. When we have anger skills, we can create a new life that is more peaceful and fulfilling.

Chapter 5

Anger our Friend

Because we may view anger as being harmful and have probably been frightened by someone's out-of-control anger, we may think it is a real stretch of the imagination to think of anger as our friend. However, our anger is purposeful and friendly because anger often alerts us to some aspect about our life that needs our attention. If we learn to listen to our anger and use anger energy for motivation to make positive changes, we will increasingly view anger as an important ally, rather than an enemy. Anger, rather than being an emotion that sabotages our life, becomes a supportive, life-fostering friend.

Anger is our friend

- Anger stands ready to provide the motivation to start what we need to start, finish what we need to finish, stop what we need to stop, release what we need to release, confront what we need to confront, clean what we need to clean, repair what we need to repair, move ourselves out of "park" and go forward with our life.
- Anger asks us to stop, listen, pay attention, and speak up about something that needs to change in our lives, such as

Anger and Guilt

being emotionally abused in a relationship.
- Anger provides energy and strength to defend ourselves or escape when we are in physical danger.
- Anger is a stage in the *grieving* process that helps us emotionally recover from loss. Unresolved grief is linked to emotional and physical illness. Actively working with our anger in the grieving process can actually prevent physical illness.
- Anger reminds us that our irrational thinking may be generating unnecessary anger.
- Anger challenges us to identify our controlling and self-serving behaviors.
- Anger alerts us when we create our own anger by having unrealistic expectations of others.
- Anger provides energy that can be directed into creating healthy change.
- When being proactive rather than reactive with our anger, we can use our anger for motivation to make good decisions for ourselves and take positive action.
- Anger provides motivation and energy to detach or leave a dysfunctional relationship.
- Most societal reforms start with the anger energy that is generated when people experience injustice and oppression.
- Anger might send an alarm to us that we have an accumulation of anger from our childhood because we lived in a dysfunctional home.
- Anger alerts us to problematic issues in our current adult relationships.
- Anger provides motivation to confront and work for changes or to take an unpopular, but morally right position, despite opposition.
- Learning anger skills and dealing with conflict peacefully

within our families is what we can do as individuals to help to achieve peace in our world.

Treating anger as a friend has other benefits. We will be able to identify and separate present anger from suppressed past anger. In relationships, if our legitimate anger is spoken in an assertive way, we will usually gain respect from others as well as gain more respect for ourselves. When we express our anger assertively, we are being our own self-advocate when we are being used or abused in relationships. Having an understanding of anger and using anger skills, we will naturally evolve to higher energy levels and experience greater satisfaction in life.

Key Points:

1. Anger stands ready to provide motivation to make positive changes in our life.
2. Healthy anger is purposeful and provides us with information and motivation to do our emotional work or self-advocate when we are being harmed.
3. Anger asks us to stop, listen, pay attention, and speak up about something that needs to change in our lives, such as being emotionally abused in a relationship.
4. Learning anger skills and dealing with conflict peacefully within our families is important if we are to be an active participant in achieving peace in our world.

Part II:

Guilt Our Foe and Friend

Chapter 6

The Powerful Emotion of Guilt

Guilt is a human emotion, and like all of our feelings, guilt is a source of information for us. When we do not acknowledge our guilt, we are denying a feeling. When we deny one feeling, we are not as aware of our other feelings. *Valid* guilt communicates to us that our behaviors are not measuring up to personal standards or values. We have done something wrong by acts of commission or we have *not* done something that we should have done, which are acts of omission. Healthy guilt is our conscience directing us to make amends for past abusive, insensitive, or inappropriate behaviors, and change behaviors that are harmful to ourselves or others. If we have no guilt when we have harmed others, we will continue our cruel behaviors and have no intention or motivation to correct our abusive actions.

Internal standards, held in our conscience, reflect parental, social, religious, moral, and spiritual standards. Our conscience prompts us to take responsibility for our actions and live in alignment with our values. Our *valid guilt* has its origins in a healthy conscience, which is developed in the first years of life, by bonding to a responsible care-taker who provides consistent nurturing. The bonding process is compromised when children are deprived of consistent care or are emotionally or physically neglected or abused. These children are more likely to have pervasive anger, act out anger in aggressive ways, and have little or no remorse about their behaviors that are harmful to others.

Besides valid guilt, there is guilt that we accept from controlling persons and guilt generated by irrational beliefs rather than from actual wrongdoing. Learning to deal with our guilt is not about sidestepping valid guilt, but rather objectively assessing the guilt to see if it is valid or invalid. An important guilt strategy is to separate real guilt from toxic guilt and discard the guilt that is irrational and not rooted in truth or reality.

People describe guilt as a pervasive tugging, aching, haunting, discontented, and gnawing feeling. Guilt is an emotion that can weigh heavily on our spirit, make us feel unworthy, and hinder or block out positive feelings such as joy, enthusiasm, and gratitude. We are adversely affected mentally, emotionally, spiritually, and physically if we allow guilt to oppress us for long periods of time. Because guilt is a powerful emotion that can be detrimental to our lives, we need to examine this emotion when it is experienced, to determine whether the guilt is *valid* or whether it is toxic guilt that needs to be eliminated from our thoughts and emotions.

Responses to the feeling of guilt

There are different responses to the feeling of guilt, and many people function in opposite positions, rather than being rational and responsible. The following are descriptions of ways that people respond to guilt. Obviously, the healthiest way of handling the feeling of guilt is the middle position, which is Position B.

The Powerful Emotion of Guilt

Position A	Position B	Position C
The guilt is not acknowledged.	**The guilt is acknowledged and responded to in healthy and responsible ways.**	**The guilt is excessive.**
These people feel they have no reason to feel guilty and do not take responsibility for their hurtful behaviors that are harmful to themselves or others.	These people make mistakes and take responsibility, but reject unrealistic, irrational, or excessive guilt. They refuse to take on guilt that is directed toward them by controllers.	These people feel guilty too frequently and are not aware of how they accept toxic guilt from others and generate their own guilt by irrational thinking.
Action Taken: Amends are seldom made because there is an unwillingness to admit fault.	**Action Taken:** These people readily make amends when they have harmed someone.	**Action Taken:** These people apologize too frequently, and often for no valid reason.

Position A: Using this approach, people do not acknowledge their guilt and, consequently, do not make amends. They are dishonest with themselves and others and, therefore, do not take responsibility for their actions. Position A is driven by pride, grandiosity, and ego, which creates an unwillingness to admit that they have harmed others. These people often think that there is either a one-up or one-down power position, and making amends is viewed as being in a one-down position. Taking a one-down power position is equated with defeat, so there is an unwillingness to apologize. We may know, or have read about persons who create fear and deep suffering in other persons' lives, seemingly without remorse, and refuse to make apologies and/or restitution.

Position C: In this position, people *burden themselves with guilt* and often generate and internalize *unhealthy, toxic, neurotic* guilt. Toxic guilt is unnecessarily experienced because it is rooted in irrational, faulty thinking. In Position C, people are self-punishing and all too willing to accept the blame from others. They apologize too frequently, even though they have done nothing wrong. Their personal boundaries are too weak, and they accept the guilt that is projected on them, which is exactly what controllers want them to do.

Healthy Position B: These people are emotionally healthy and have a well-developed conscience. In Position B, the cause of guilt is determined and action is taken. Efforts are made to change behaviors when internal standards have not been met. When there is actual wrongdoing, amends are made. Manipulative, controlling guilt messages are rejected and are often confronted. Irrational guilt is dismissed. In this position, there is clear thinking and honesty, and responding to *valid* guilt in responsible and appropriate ways.

What we learned about guilt as children

As children, we may have had parents who made us feel guilty in various situations. Guilt is often used to make children be compliant and do what parents want them to do, which may be something reasonable or unreasonable. Children are often made to feel guilty when unintentionally spilling, breaking, or making other messes, often caused by their fine and gross motor skills, which are not fully developed. If children are involved in family arguments and chaos, they may feel responsible and, as a result, feel guilty. Children feel excessive guilt if they are constantly told that they are a burden or that everything is their fault. Recalling childhood experiences may uncover many times when we were told as children "shame on you" even though our behaviors were not bad, but were the behaviors of healthy children.

When we are young, we have no way to reject toxic guilt. As children, we accepted the guilt, which lowered our self-esteem. If we experienced frequent guilt, we were set up for being less likely to self-actualize and share our talents and resources with others. In essence, the world lost what we were meant to contribute, because of false and toxic guilt. Years later, we may be carrying the guilt imposed on us by parents. However, as adults, we have the choice of accepting or rejecting controlling guilt when we realize that no one can make us feel inadequate and guilty without our consent.

Valid guilt sends a message

- **Guilt because of actual wrongdoing**. This type of guilt, when experienced by healthy people, creates a feeling of responsibility and remorse, which are the appropriate feelings when we have committed *actual wrongdoing*. Rational, valid guilt is a result of abusive behaviors such as:
  - Physically, sexually, verbally, mentally, or emotionally harming others
  - Controlling others with manipulation, unjust criticisms, and sarcastic put-downs
  - Failing to be a responsible adult
  - Damaging or destroying property
  - Being dishonest
  - Physically, emotionally, mentally, or spiritually harming *ourselves*

Valid, real, and authentic guilt sends a message that we need to acknowledge our wrongdoing, take responsibility, and make amends or restitution to the person we have harmed. When we experience valid guilt, we are prompted to examine our actions so that we do not repeat the same harmful behavior toward ourselves or others.

- ❖ **Survivor guilt** involves feeling guilty for escaping harm or death while others suffered or died. This type of guilt sends a message to reach out to help others less fortunate and actualize ourselves so that we are more able to advocate for change when there is injustice. Survivor guilt also teaches us to be grateful for our blessings in life.
- ❖ **Existential guilt** is caused by:
    - ✓ Not being all that we can be because of reasons such as being fearful, not believing in ourselves, lack of motivation, or refusing to take risks
    - ✓ Not taking care of ourselves physically, mentally, emotionally, and spiritually
    - ✓ Being unclear on the purpose of our life and focusing on acquiring possessions and social status
    - ✓ Not being grateful for having a higher quality of life than others
    - ✓ Not changing over-consuming behaviors that cause scarcity for others

Existential guilt challenges us to ponder the meaning of our existence and direct our energies toward what we discover to be the purpose of our lives. Existential guilt challenges us to confront wrong actions, work for global peace and justice, share our resources with people who are struggling because of natural or manmade disasters, and find ways to advocate for those who are powerless and have no voice in the decisions that affect their lives. This type of valid guilt signals us to think about a decision that might be harmful to others, too extravagant, unfair, or is self-indulgent at the expense of others. Existential guilt prompts us to recognize the interconnectedness of all people and take personal responsibility for making a positive contribution to the world.

- **The guilt of self-betrayal** communicates to us that we betray ourselves when we enable rather than confront emotionally abusive behaviors; when we sacrifice our beliefs and values; or when any of our behaviors are contrary to our internal beliefs and principles, such as not walking our talk. The healthy guilt message is to respect and honor the self and live by our internal beliefs and ethical principles.
- **Guilt when we are not being responsible**. If we under-function and expect others to do our work, guilt will knock at our internal doorstep. By not doing what we are capable of doing, by blaming others and making excuses for our irresponsible behaviors, and by acting like an impulsive, self-centered, and attention-seeking child, we are apt to feel the guilt of being irresponsible. The healthy guilt message is to step up and perform according to the normal expectations of adulthood, stop under-functioning and expecting others to over-function, work productively according to abilities, strengths, and talents, and take our share of responsibility when there are problems.

Being irresponsible also involves behaviors that are harmful to ourselves or others. If we are doing any activity excessively and obsessively, such as using mood-altering substances, gambling, or playing violent video games, we are likely to feel valid guilt. The guilt message encourages us to change behaviors that are excessive and over-stimulating or, in contrast, stagnate our minds and take time away from meaningful relationships. If we are neglecting ourselves, such as not exercising, we are likely to feel guilty. Guilt reminds us to honor the gift of life we have been given by taking good care of ourselves.

When we fail to use basic interpersonal skills in relationships, such as being honest, respectful, attentive, and good listeners, guilt will have a message for us. If we do not share our loving feelings in relationships of significance or if we failed to do or say something to someone who died, we are likely to feel guilt. Guilt sends a message that encourages us to give as much as we expect to receive in relationships, take the perspective of others, reach out and emotionally connect with people, have compassion and be supportive of people who are suffering. By using this approach, the lives of the people we love will be enriched as well as our own, and we will prevent long-lasting regrets.

Some guilt thoughts remind us about the possibility of inadvertently harming a child while driving a vehicle, or causing harm or strife to others created by our negligence or high-risk behaviors. The healthy guilt message is to be cautious, sober, and refrain from reckless behaviors that could lead to harming ourselves or others.

We need to keep in mind that valid, healthy guilt that is taken to extreme becomes toxic and, therefore, detrimental to our overall well-being. Common sense needs to prevail. Our task is to hear the guilt message and listen to the advice that guilt sends to us. Our guilt lessons will return repeatedly until we change our thoughts, beliefs, or behaviors to be more positive and life-enhancing.

Invalid, toxic guilt is life-diminishing

❖ **Guilt that we accept from controlling persons is toxic guilt**

If we take on the guilt that controlling people project on us, we can become overwhelmed with feelings of guilt. Accepting guilt from others is more likely to happen when we have low self-esteem and weak personal boundaries. We internalize guilt that is projected on us, act out of a feeling of obligation rather than choice, and end up feeling resentful. A common thought is that complying with someone's requests is easier than dealing with the guilt we would feel if we did not comply.

Examples of taking on the guilt that does not belong to us:

- ✓ When we readily accept toxic and controlling guilt messages given to us by parents, spouses, friends, employers, and religious, legal, welfare, or other social systems
- ✓ When we comply with the requests or demands of controlling people who make us feel guilty, even though we have other time commitments, priorities, beliefs, and relationships
- ✓ When children are made to feel guilty because of the unrealistic expectations of adults regarding their behaviors and achievements
- ✓ When we are abused and take on the guilt that rightfully belongs to the perpetrator

- Cynthia shares:

    For years, I thought I was at fault for being sexually assaulted because I had forgotten to lock my apartment. Every day I would scold myself. I would think about how dumb I was and that the assault was my fault. I felt ashamed and hated myself. Then the nightmares came, and that's when I had to reach out for help. My therapist was very supportive, and finally I started realizing that I didn't cause the assault and that, similar to what other victims do, I was taking on the blame and guilt. Now I look back at those days and wonder how my thinking could be so mixed up. It's a miracle that I'm alive to tell my story and share how the assault made me feel.

❖ **Guilt generated by irrational beliefs rather from actual wrongdoing is toxic guilt**

Guilt based on irrational thoughts and beliefs is guilt that is experienced, but there has been no actual wrongdoing. Because of irrational thinking, we generate guilt that causes our faults and fears to take center stage in our lives. One common way of thinking irrationally is comparing ourselves to a *standard of perfection* that may involve:

- our physical appearance
- the amount of work we do
- the number of friends we have
- the amount of money and possessions we have
- how intelligent we are
- our achievements
- how religious we are

When we compare ourselves to a standard of perfection, we feel inferior and guilty because in our minds, we can never be perfect or good enough. This is irrational, faulty thinking and is usually not in our conscious awareness. When we are not aware that our thinking is faulty, we keep repeating the same self-sabotaging thoughts. Guilt can become a habit, similar to an addiction. Like any addiction, we are restless, irritable, and discontent. We can feel guilty for so long, and to such an extreme, that we compromise our emotional and mental health.

People say, "My life is run by guilt. I feel guilty about a lot of things, like not doing enough or not wanting to be with people who are always complaining." Or, "I feel guilty when I make little mistakes, like forgetting to buy milk at the grocery store." These types of statements reflect a harsh inner critic, which is the nagging, negative voice that speaks silently to us. Our inner critic echoes the statements of dysfunctional parents, siblings, teachers, peers, clergy, or other people who conditioned us into thinking we were inadequate and innately inferior. Our inner critic is a nasty menace that chatters in our heads, creates guilt, and makes us feel unlovable and worthless. Our self-esteem is diminished and we can become vulnerable to depression, anxiety, self-injurious behavior, eating disorders, and addictions. The inner critic fades into the background as we reject false guilt, use positive self-talk, and grow in self-esteem.

Guilt is our foe...

- When we are victimized and take on the guilt that rightfully belongs to the perpetrator
- When we accept, internalize, and harbor guilt messages from others
- When guilt feelings are contrary to logic
- When we feel guilty for not being perfect
- When our irrational guilt sabotages our self-esteem, creates feelings of self-doubt and unworthiness, and sabotages our emotional health

◄ Anger and Guilt

- When guilt feelings remain even after we have apologized
- When guilt is used for emotionally punishing ourselves
- When we allow ourselves to be victims of guilt and not move on with our lives
- When we feel guilty for things that are beyond our control
- When we are dishonest and make false excuses because of our guilt
- When chronic guilt contributes to physical illness, such as skin disorders, auto-immune disorders, arthritis, digestive disorders, headaches, fibromyalgia, and/or excessive fatigue.

I feel guilty about:

My guilt feels like:

Guilt is our friend...

- When guilt signals to us that we're not living up to our own standards and expectations of ourselves
- When guilt alerts us to actual wrongdoing and prompts us to take responsibility and make amends
- When our guilt alerts us to our faulty ways of thinking that need changing to be more reality-based and life-fostering
- When we feel good for taking positive action for the right reasons
- When guilt reminds us to be more honest with ourselves and others

- When guilt prompts us to help disadvantaged people and disaster victims in whatever way that we are able
- When our guilt directs us to prevent future regrets by choosing to be with someone who is difficult but may only be with us for a short period of time
- When our guilt signals us to think about a decision that might be wrong, too extravagant, unfair, or is self-indulgent at the expense of others
- When guilt encourages us to consider the needs of others and be more caring
- When guilt sends a message to take our share of responsibility when problems arise in relationships
- When guilt is a motivator to change unhealthy or addictive behaviors that negatively affect ourselves and others
- When the discomfort of guilt helps us to learn from negative experiences so we don't repeat behaviors that harm ourselves or others

Key Points:

1. Our *valid guilt* has its origins in a healthy conscience, which is developed in the first years of life by bonding to a responsible care-taker who provides consistent nurturing.
2. When we carry guilt for long periods of time, we become vulnerable to physical illness such as skin disorders, auto-immune disorders, arthritis, digestive disorders, headaches, fibromyalgia, and/or excessive fatigue.
3. The major forms of guilt are rational guilt, which is rooted in a healthy conscience, the guilt that we accept from controlling persons, or irrational, false guilt, which is created by faulty thinking.

4. Guilt is our foe when it is irrational, toxic, and excessive.
5. Guilt is our friend when it prompts us to take responsibility for our actions, change unhealthy behaviors, and make amends if we have harmed others.

Chapter 7

Guilt Used to Control Others

Guilt, similar to aggressive anger, is a common way of controlling others, either by taking a one-up or a one-down position. The **one-up position** is taken by acting superior and making statements about the other person's inadequacy and incompetency to put them in a one-down position.

Controller takes a one-up position by posing as superior and more powerful

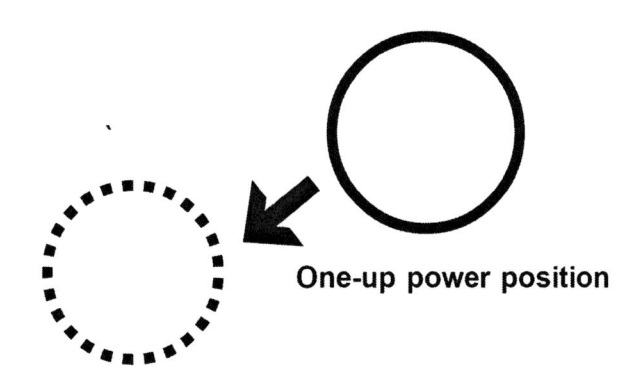

One-up power position

One - down less powerful position

◄ Anger and Guilt

In this diagram the controller takes a superior, one-up position to get compliance from another person. We can easily identify the controllers in our lives by thinking about the people we are tempted to be dishonest with, or we actually tell lies or make up false excuses to prevent conflict and avoid doing something we don't want to do. Controllers are those people in our lives we would like to escape from because we feel obligated to comply with their requests. Often, we feel that we are being held hostage in a relationship with a controller. Controllers who use the one-up position to control others prey on persons who are nice, non-confronting, compassionate, and who are willing to make sacrifices in relationships at the expense of themselves. What recipients of control benefit from learning is that just because someone tries to put us in a one-down, inferior position doesn't mean we have to go there, unless there is a safety concern.

Controllers who take a **<u>one-up</u>** power position to instill guilt in others:

- ✓ Do not respect others' personal rights, such as the right to make one's own choices
- ✓ Blame others and make false or exaggerated accusations to instill guilt
- ✓ Know that by presenting themselves as powerful and making others feel guilty, they are likely to get their requests met
- ✓ Present themselves as having the right way, and others are inferior and inadequate
- ✓ Are likely to have little understanding, nor do they care about how they place others in awkward, uncomfortable, and obligatory positions

Typical statements from a <u>one-up</u> position intended to instill guilt in others:

You are never here when I need you.
If you really loved me, you would know what to do.
If you had a brain, this wouldn't have happened!
You have to work late...again?
We are broke again? Where are you spending all the money?
No supper made? What have you been doing all day?
I can never depend on you! You are always screwing things up!
You're going to visit your friend...again?
You are so stubborn!
You are lazy and good for nothing...a total joke!

These put-down statements are often accepted and internalized by people who accept the controlling guilt, and are often successful in getting the other person to respond out of guilt.

Guilt can also be projected on others by taking a **<u>one-down</u>** position. This is posturing as being helpless or being a victim because of others' insensitivity or uncaring. Guilt is projected on others to get compliance from another person, which is commonly known as the *guilt-trip*.

Controller takes a one-down position and manipulates by posing as weak to get compliance

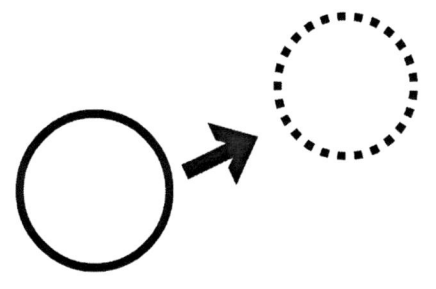

Controller takes a one-down power position to get compliance

◄ Anger and Guilt

In this diagram the controller takes a one-down position, acting helpless or being victimized because of others' insensitivity or uncaring. A guilt-trip is put on others in order to get compliance to requests. An example of a one-down statement is, "I can't possibly pay you because I have so many other bills." The unspoken message is that the other person is insensitive because they expect to be paid by someone who is financially over-burdened and helpless to do anything about it. By taking a one-down position, the recipient of the guilt will often agree or comply because of feeling guilty and obligated.

Controllers, who take a **one-down** position to instill guilt in others:

- ✓ Make others believe that they will suffer if others do not meet their demands
- ✓ Pose as helpless, innocent, and virtuous victims
- ✓ Imply that other people are unkind, unsympathetic, and uncaring if they do not comply with their requests
- ✓ Imply that negative consequences could happen. They may threaten to become sick, have a heart attack, remove someone from their last will and testament, or give up on life if requests are not met with compliance.

Typical statements from a <u>one-down</u> position to instill guilt in others:

You expect me to do all that?
I haven't heard from you for so long, I thought you died.
But when you're gone, I'm all alone with nothing to do.
Don't make supper… I'll just eat cereal!
I am so unhappy and you seem to be happy every day!

Go ahead; take the last morsel of food. I haven't eaten today, but enjoy!
You're not coming home for Christmas?
You are the only person I can talk to, but you are always doing other things.
I feel badly, but I don't think you even care.

Guilt-making controllers, who are apt to be dependent and expect others to do things for them, need guilt-takers who will accept the guilt. When controllers manipulate by using guilt, they seem to *make* us feel guilty because we do not realize that we have a choice as to whether or not to feel guilty. Controlling persons take advantage of nice, caring, and friendly people who act out of obligation rather than choice. People who are controlled by guilt often compromise their physical, mental, emotional, or spiritual selves, which include their values, beliefs, and goals. They often become emotionally dishonest to prevent conflicts, and say "yes" when they really want to say "no." What is important to learn is that just because someone tries to put us in a one-down, inferior position doesn't mean we have to give up our power and be compliant. We have a right to make healthy choices for ourselves.

Guilt-making, controlling behaviors are often enabled

Controlling behaviors are often enabled in order to prevent conflict. Enabling stems from good intentions, but results in fueling the controlling behaviors. People comply with a controller's requests because they don't want to be viewed as someone who is mean, selfish, and uncaring. However, enabling is helping the controller to be successful in their controlling, guilt-making behaviors. When we enable, we allow, accommodate, adjust, comply, protect, sacrifice preferences and dreams, and pretend that everything is fine when everything is not fine.

We enable when we accept guilt that doesn't belong to us and feel guilty although we have nothing to feel guilty about. We are often over-responsible and bend over backwards to meet controllers' requests. We think that it is easier to do something for the other person than feel guilty. We often compromise our mental, emotional, and physical health and martyr ourselves. We are highly invested in keeping the peace and making everyone happy. Despite all of our efforts, we live with guilt and seldom realize that it is **toxic, irrational** guilt because it has nothing to do with actual wrongdoing.

Controllers, whether they use anger or guilt to control, usurp the energies of other people, but are never truly satisfied with what is given to them. Regardless of how others comply, support, nurture, or provide, it is never enough and often, never *good* enough. When this realization becomes crystal clear, the recipients of control are likely to start developing refusal skills so that they are not acting in ways that are contrary to their beliefs, priorities, values, and interests.

- Tom shares:

    My controller had her ways to get me to submit to her wishes by putting a guilt-trip on me. If I didn't do certain things, I would feel guilty, so it was easier to do them. This could involve things like never going anywhere without her, or spending a week with her relatives who drank a lot, which bothered me. I have learned that if I take on the guilt, it is a choice I make. So I am no longer a guilt taker. Interestingly, I think my wife respects me more for confronting her when she tries to make me feel guilty. So my getting clearer about guilt has helped us both, and our relationship is better.

The many forms of enabling guilt-making control

- **Allowing** is being silent, rather than confronting when we are experiencing guilt trips put on us, which is helping guilt tactics to be successful.
- **Accommodating** is trying to meet the controller's numerous expectations, and if we are unsuccessful in pleasing the guilt-making controller, we feel guilty. We internalize the controller's guilt statements and fail to set limits on what is acceptable and what is not acceptable.
- **Adjusting** is changing plans to go along with the controller's plans so we don't feel guilty.
- **Complying** is doing what controllers want us to do to pacify them. We are compliant to prevent, avoid, or stop a hassle, try to do things perfectly, agree when we really want to disagree, and participate in disliked or uninteresting activities to prevent feeling guilty. We want to be viewed as cooperative and friendly people and continually respond to requests because of toxic guilt.
- **Sacrificing preferences and dreams** is placing more importance on the controller's preferences and dreams than our own; not actualizing our life regarding our work or personal development because we think it would be selfish; or "psyching up" to be nice, pleasing, and tolerant of the controller. These are all efforts to avoid feeling guilty.

Enabling manipulative guilt tactics probably began in childhood. These were our best efforts to prevent disapproving responses from parents, to be accepted and loved, or sometimes, to survive. We may have tried to be the perfect child. Many of us were dishonest in efforts to hide our mistakes. We may have been shamed for doing child-like activities such as splashing in puddles, not eating all of the food that was put on our plate, or spilling spaghetti sauce on our shirt. Now that we are adults, our personal empowerment involves identifying guilt tactics and dismissing the guilt that was perhaps inadvertently, but wrongly put upon us.

Responding to one-up, one-down manipulative, controlling tactics

Controllers who use one-up, one-down tactics overlook the fact that there is a neutral, middle, assertive position, which is increasingly being understood and used by people who refuse to be manipulated. When controllers use guilt, a person can respond to the controller by taking a neutral position, rather than being manipulated by one-up or one-down statements. As a result, controllers are often unsure of what to do because their control maneuvers are not working. Refusing to be controlled is easier to do when the controller uses guilt, as opposed to aggressive anger, which creates a potential for physical danger.

Cultural socialization generates toxic guilt

Social conditioning promotes stereotypes, which are a set of directives as to what males and females *should* think and feel, and how each gender is to behave. Stereotypes are not truth, but are presented as truth in advertisements, movies, songs, and other media. Though we may not be aware of the socialization process and how it affects our lives, we are very aware of what it is to behave like a male or behave like a female. When we don't live up to our assigned stereotypes, we often feel guilty.

Guilt Used to Control Others

A sampling of male stereotypes:

- Be strong and productive.
- Be good at problem-solving and base your decisions on logical thought.
- Don't be emotional and if you have feelings, don't express them.
- Crying is not okay.
- Be independent and dominant in relationships.
- Be aggressive, powerful and conquer.
- Your opinions are important and are correct.
- Never walk away from competition.
- Be bold, brave, and in control.
- Fix things that don't work.
- Make things happen.

A sampling of female stereotypes:

- Be nurturing and care-taking of others.
- Make adjustments and be accommodating.
- Be weak, adaptable, passive, compliant, selfless, nice, passive, and attractive.
- Please others.
- Your decisions and opinions are inferior because they are based on feelings and intuition.
- Don't rock the boat, don't feel important, and don't complain or criticize.
- Don't be so emotional.
- Don't be angry.
- Don't talk about anything sad or too deep.
- Don't challenge others' viewpoints or behaviors.
- Don't be too intelligent or competent.

Anger and Guilt

Acting in stereotypical ways results in social approval, while acting in ways that are contrary to stereotypical directives often results in being criticized and viewed as inadequate. As we grow in our awareness, we move beyond functioning within stereotypical expectations because we realize that stereotypes are only characteristics designed to be supportive of more powerful people. Many of us, in our society, can make the choice to reject predetermined descriptions and patterns of behavior that do not fit us or that we know are unhealthy. We are not going to be struck dead if we reject the negative and life-diminishing directives that we learned from our culture. They are only constructs, blueprints, theories, or designs that are set forth as truth, but are not truth. We are not bound to them, nor do we need to feel guilty if we do not live according to cultural stereotypes, expectations, and directives.

Socialization creates separateness. Though there have been some changes within our society, men are socialized with expectations that they need to be right, know everything, never show feelings, and be in competition with others. Women are socialized into believing that men's ways are superior and that women's priorities and ways of relating have less value. *Both* genders are oppressed if they follow and adhere to societal expectations and feel guilty if they don't meet gender descriptions. With increased awareness and personal growth, men will realize that showing feelings is not a sign of weakness, nor a reason to feel guilty. Women will realize that they are not always wrong or inferior and that much of the guilt they feel is totally irrational.

We sacrifice honesty when we respond to guilt messages and agree to behave in ways that are contrary to our beliefs, values, and priorities. Whether controllers use anger or guilt to control and manipulate, we enable the control when we compromise ourselves. Being dishonest and sacrificing our beliefs, values, and priorities are contrary to spiritual principles.

We lose our authentic self when we let guilt direct our choices and actions. We will not achieve personal growth to higher levels of thinking or embrace who we really are— emotionally, mentally, and spiritually—if we remain a victim to our irrational guilt. Rather than increasingly becoming self-actualized persons, our personal growth and our relationships are put at risk. In addition, we become messengers to the next generation, passing on false information that generates guilt.

We cannot experience wholeness if we allow ourselves to be victims of guilt that is projected on us or generated by our irrational thinking and beliefs. Whether we are male or female, we will not be able to love ourselves or feel peace within ourselves if irrational, toxic guilt is directing our lives. Rather than thinking we are inferior, unworthy, and that feeling guilty is virtuous, we can refuse to be guilt receptacles. We can sort through our guilt, discard toxic guilt, and if the guilt is valid, make amends. We can then move on to a higher level of well-being by being responsible, authentic, proactive, and evolving human beings.

Women and Guilt

Women are not very good at feeling angry, but they are very good at feeling guilty. Many women are bogged down by irrational, needless, invalid guilt. Women are expected to be passive, understanding, compassionate, helpful, empathetic, and willing to alter schedules, preferences, priorities, and activities in order to meet others' needs or requests. Women often try to be a twenty-four-hour, one-stop shopping mall, having whatever is needed for anyone who makes a request. Since women are viewed in our culture as responsible for making relationships work, there is guilt if their relationships deteriorate. If husbands have affairs or leave the marriage, the

◄ Anger and Guilt

blame is often placed on women. When this happens, many women readily take on the toxic guilt that is life-diminishing.

Since women are socialized to be nurturers, they often comply with others' demands in efforts to make everything go smoothly and not upset anyone. Many women feel guilty for confronting, disagreeing, being angry, or refusing to be over-extended. When women start refusing to accept guilt, and stop doing things for people that they should be doing for themselves, they are often called selfish, uncooperative, and stubborn, as a manipulative way to have them return to their passive behaviors. Because of pressure from societal messages and from their personal relationships, women are frequently too willing to neglect themselves and use their energy to nurture others.

It is not uncommon that when women demonstrate their personal power, the outcome is feeling guilty because of criticism from men and often from other women. In administrative positions, where there can be difficult decisions to make regarding people's lives, such as having to terminate someone from their employment, women walk a fine line between acting decisively and still being responsive to the expectation that they be emotionally warm and nurturing. So often, when women need to be firm and decisive, they feel guilty and alienated from others.

Though changes are happening, women are still considered to be the main caretaker in the family. Mothers feel guilty when bringing their children to day-care, feel guilty when their children have behavior or learning problems, and feel responsible and guilty when their children experiment with alcohol and drugs and become sexually active at an early age and before marriage. Women feel guilty when the house isn't orderly, the laundry piles are high, the garbage is overflowing, and when there is no milk in the refrigerator. When fathers are distant or controlling, many mothers try desperately to make up for the nurturing their children do not receive from their fathers and feel guilty when they are not successful. And often, all of this guilt is hidden within them and is never discussed with others. The accumulated guilt may cause emotional, physical, and spiritual harm. If women eliminated all of the actions prompted by their guilt, there would be time and energy to put efforts into their own goals, which are likely to include making their own choices and actualizing their potential.

- Meghan shares:

   I felt guilty when my husband would do some of the housework, even though I had asked him to do it, because we both worked. I watched him do laundry and cringed with guilt, even though I was telling myself that I had no reason to feel guilty! Why I keep doing this to myself, I don't know. I am a pretty intelligent person, but can't seem to let go of my crazy guilt!

Religious guilt

Some organized religions emphasize the sinfulness and unworthiness of humans, and that people should not question religious teachings. These two messages are highly controlling. Guilt is a common feeling if we believe that God watches for mistakes and punishes transgressors during this lifetime and in the eternal damnation of hell. If we accept the doctrine of original sin, which is not Scripture based, we are bound to feel that we are innately sinful and cannot do anything to change this fact. Guilt permeates our thoughts if we are taught in our religious tradition that we are not good enough, do not believe enough, that we don't pray enough, and don't give enough. People readily share that they go to church services just to avoid feeling guilty. Many people feel guilty when they question and subsequently reject some of their religious teachings. Based on their experience with what is taught in organized religion, many people struggle with religious guilt, which contributes to low self-esteem, self-punishing and negating oneself, and thinking that God's love is earned by being perfect. Examples of religious guilt are:

- Feeling guilty about having normal human thoughts and desires
- Feeling guilty for anything involved with the physical body (the "flesh")
- Feeling guilty because of being told they are very sinful even though they are trying to be good people
- Feeling guilty for not praying enough, not practicing sacrificial giving, not being religious enough, and not feeling connected to God
- Feeling guilty when not attending religious services

- Cheri shares:

   What I experience about most Christian religions is the huge presence of guilt, which was noticeably absent in the Native and Hawaiian spirituality, before the advent of the Christians. Having been brought up as a Christian, I sometimes say to myself, "How do we DARE go through life without a load of guilt?" And, yet, my soul tells me to be at peace because my God loves me and doesn't enjoy making us jump through hoops to be saved. Something tells me that those are concepts developed by men, and I do mean men by gender, to somehow keep the strength of women in line. So, I have this running argument with my brother's wife, who believes that the Bible is the inspired Word of God and must be believed verbatim, including the verses about homosexuals in the Old Testament. She thinks I am bound for RUIN, but I am at PEACE with my God.

- Mel shares:

    I've struggled with religious guilt all my life! The nuns were always telling us we were doing things wrong, and I always felt guilty. Now I realize their negative responses to us did not follow Christ's true message. For years, I thought I was going to hell because I ate meat on a Friday by mistake, and another time I chewed gum on a fasting day. I feel that many young people, including myself, were emotionally battered, and it took a long time to heal our wounds and recover some semblance of self-esteem. God only knows how the sexually abused are doing, and I pray for their healing. I am quite sure that everyone has still not recovered!

- Lonnie shares:

    I used to feel guilty a lot, but now I understand where it came from. I learned to feel guilty from my parents and from the Catholic nuns who were my teachers. My friends and I often talk about our Catholic guilt. Looking back at our elementary school years, I feel that we were all emotionally abused. We started with joy in our hearts and spirits, but were forced to be disciplined, quiet, and somber. Our joy was replaced by bad feelings about ourselves.

For many people, guilt seems to come along with the Catholic faith, and they feel guilty for many reasons, including practicing birth control, divorcing, self-pleasuring, and marrying a non-Catholic. But it is not only the Catholic religious tradition that promotes unhealthy guilt. Lutherans and Jewish people have many of the same guilt feelings that are rooted in their religious tradition. Even ministers struggle with guilt:

- Elton shares:

   > I am a Lutheran pastor, and I am finally living without overwhelming guilt. It took me years to realize that most of my guilt was based on false teachings, which were designed to control people. I feel that I am liberated from toxic guilt, and it is like being born again. I refuse to teach my parishioners that God is an angry and punishing God that wants us to be burdened with guilt or a negative opinion of ourselves. When we are beaten down and have low self-esteem, we will hesitate to reach out and serve others in healthy ways, which is what we are supposed to do as Christians.

Emotional liberation and freedom

Feeling guilty doesn't always mean that we have something to feel guilty about. Our emotional liberation and freedom involve freeing ourselves from any false constructs, dogmas, cultural expectations, religious guilt, the guilt projected by controllers, or ways of thinking that are irrational. Toxic guilt is a hindrance to mental, emotional, physical, and spiritual growth. An important part of an empowering process is erasing, removing, and discarding what we have learned that is false, negative, and detrimental to our emotional health. Gaining clarity on the feeling of guilt is not only beneficial for ourselves, but also for our children, who may learn to respond *only* to healthy, valid guilt.

What guilt is directly related to my cultural conditioning?

What guilt comes from my religious upbringing?

How is guilt affecting my life?

What changes do I need to make in my thoughts and beliefs?

How do I enable the guilt that is used to control me?

In order to give up my guilt I would have to:

My current guilt challenge:

Keys Points:

1. The guilt that controllers project on others to manipulate and control is not valid guilt because there is no actual wrongdoing.
2. If we accept and enable guilt manipulations, the control will continue.
3. If we have the freedom and personal power to make our own choices, we can reject the harmful, guilt-producing aspects of socialization.
4. If we accept controllers' guilt, we are likely to compromise our values, beliefs, and priorities.
5. Our emotional liberation and freedom involve discarding false constructs, dogmas, directives, and expectations that are controlling and life-diminishing.

Chapter 8

Responding to Valid Guilt

When we have emotionally, mentally, sexually, or physically abused others, vandalized property, or committed other illegal acts, guilt is the appropriate feeling. However, there are people who intentionally avoid, deny, or defend their abusive behaviors and claim innocence. When observing people, it becomes apparent that those who should feel guilty often do not feel guilty, in contrast to many victims, who take on the guilt that rightfully belongs to perpetrators.

Unhealthy ways of dealing with <u>valid</u>, <u>rational</u> guilt

- **Staying in denial about the valid guilt.** When we are in denial, we do not acknowledge our harmful actions. When challenged, we become defensive, change the topic, discredit the one confronting, justify inappropriate behaviors, or suppress the guilt. By not acknowledging our guilt, we excuse ourselves and do not change behaviors or make amends or restitution. In a one-up, one-down way of thinking, making amends is viewed as taking a one-down position. There is resistance to taking a one-down position because it is often equated with being defeated and powerless.
- **Putting the guilt on others and justifying the wrong**

action. This is accusing others of causing or *bringing on* the harmful behaviors. The wrong action is justified by distorting or exaggerating information. Statements are made such as, "You didn't fix supper so I lost my temper and hit you! Or, "You started it, so I finished it!" These types of statements put the guilt on others as a way to excuse the abusive behaviors. Rather than taking personal responsibility, other persons' actions are put in the spotlight. Abusive behaviors are not acknowledged.
- **Minimizing the wrongdoing.** Minimizing the wrongdoing is an effort to escape the guilt and avoid the unpleasantness of making amends. Most bullies and perpetrators will deny or minimize the emotional, physical, or sexual harm they have inflicted on their victims. Some perpetrators say that their victims did not protest the abuse, so there was no wrongdoing. Other perpetrators say that the victim invited the abuse, which is incredibly distorted thinking, as well as appalling.

The appropriate response to valid guilt is making amends

A healthy conscience creates remorse and directs us to apologize or make restitution for the harm that we caused. True remorse is not the remorse of being caught, or false remorse just to avoid punishment, but is genuine. To arrive at the point of *willingness* to apologize requires self-reflection, taking responsibility, and resolving to not repeat the mistakes that caused harm. Making amends or making restitution requires honesty, courage, and humility. Some persons cling to their pride, resist admitting their errors, and panic when they are faced with the challenge of making amends.

Checking motivations for making amends is important because apologies could be misguided and used to get us off the hook so that we feel better. Amends should have no ulterior motives. Rather, amends need to involve taking responsibility for the harmful actions, feeling truly sorry, and wanting to make things right with the person we have offended, hurt, abused, or treated unfairly. There also needs to be an acknowledgement of how the person/persons were affected. Because of our actions, they may have suffered emotionally, physically, sexually, financially, mentally, and/or spiritually. We also need to communicate that our harmful actions will never be repeated. When *serious harm* has been inflicted, making apologies and asking for forgiveness seem very inadequate, but expressing our remorse and amends may, to some degree, be emotionally helpful to those we have harmed.

The outcomes of making amends are not predictable. It is important that we have no expectations of what will happen. Expecting victims to respond enthusiastically to our amends is just another version of controlling behaviors. Some persons will be frightened to be with us because of the mistrust that was created when our behaviors were abusive. Other people may reject apologies or minimize the offense, be dishonest, and say that "it was no big deal," when it actually *was* a big deal. Some of the people that we have harmed may be intensely angry. If people refuse to meet with us, an alternative is to write a letter of apology.

Making sincere amends assures the person who was harmed that they were not at fault. The person may start the process of regaining trust, which is a risk for them that the offender needs to acknowledge. The relationship may not be fully restored, but there is potential for a considerable amount of healing if sincere amends are made. Optimally, the person who was harmed will listen and be receptive, but regardless of the other person's response, he/she needs to be treated respectfully.

Making sincere amends helps us to clear the wreckage of our past regarding what we have abusively done to others. There

◄ Anger and Guilt

is also the moral benefit of doing the right thing for the right reasons. Apologizing is an emotional *cleansing* for ourselves, as well as for the injured person and the relationship. The Twelve-Step program suggests a process for making amends. The eighth step of the Twelve-Step spiritual program is: "Made a list of all persons we had harmed, and became willing to make amends to them all." The ninth step is "Made direct amends to such people whenever possible, except when to do so would injure them or others." The tenth step is: "Continued to take personal inventory and when we were wrong promptly admitted it." The Alcoholics Anonymous book, *Twelve Steps and Twelve Traditions,* states: "Good judgment will suggest that we ought to take our time. While we may be quite willing to reveal the very worst, we must be sure to remember that we cannot buy our own peace of mind at the expense of others."

Summary — *our amends need to involve:*

- Taking full responsibility, communicating that what we did was wrong and that our feelings of guilt and remorse are sincere
- Recognizing that the victim suffered because of our harmful actions
- Making apologies that are honest, sincere, and respectful
- Making restitution if there was property damage and also offering to pay for the emotional damage or inconveniences that occurred
- Making an honest commitment to not repeat the harmful actions

If we approach making amends with honesty and sincerity, then regardless of the outcome, we have stepped forward, reached out, expressed our remorse, and made sincere apologies. If amends are not accepted, we can at least take heart in the fact that we made an attempt to promote healing within the relationship. Perhaps, after some time has passed, we may want to try making our amends again.

Acknowledging and responding to other forms of valid guilt

- **Survivor guilt** sends a message to reach out to help others who suffer and actualize ourselves so that we are more able to advocate for change when there is injustice. Survivor guilt also teaches us to be grateful for our blessings in life.
- **Existential guilt** challenges us to ponder the meaning of our existence and direct our energies toward our life-purpose. Existential guilt prompts us to recognize the interconnectedness of all people and take personal responsibility for making a positive contribution to the world. This requires a willingness to confront wrong actions, work for global peace and justice, share our resources with people who are struggling because of natural or manmade disasters, and find ways to advocate for those who are powerless and have no voice in the decisions that affect their lives. This type of valid guilt signals us to think about a decision that might be wrong, too extravagant, unfair, or is self-indulgent at the expense of others.
- **The guilt of self-betrayal** encourages us to respect and honor ourselves and develop and live up to internal standards, beliefs, and ethical principles. When we go along to get along, and our actions are a total contradiction of what we believe, our guilt prompts us to change behaviors to be in alignment with our basic values.
- **Guilt when we are not being responsible** asks us to step up and perform according to the normal expectations of adulthood; stop under-functioning and expecting others to

over-function; work productively according to our abilities, strengths, and talents; and take our share of responsibility when there are problems. If we are neglecting ourselves, such as not exercising or eating nutritiously, guilt asks us to honor the gift of life that we have been given by taking better care of ourselves. Guilt encourages us to give as much as we expect to receive in relationships, take the perspective of others, reach out and emotionally connect with people, and have compassion and be supportive of people who are suffering.

When the wrong action was in response to being harmed

It becomes more complex when dealing with the harmful actions that are in *response* to being mentally, emotionally, physically, or sexually abused. These actions are often aggressive behaviors by teenagers or adults to retaliate and inflict harm on a bully, sexual predator, or a controller who has been emotionally, verbally, or physically abusive.

Examples of actions in response to disrespectful treatment or abuse causing guilt:

- Physically harming a sexual predator
- A teenager physically fighting a parent who is yelling, screaming, and making threatening body gestures to the other parent
- Being physically or verbally abusive with a parent who has been or is currently being abusive
- Physically harming someone in self-defense

When we feel guilty for these actions, we have to consider the circumstances and think carefully as to how much guilt to accept. Though we need to take ownership of our behaviors and not excuse

Responding to Valid Guilt

ourselves, we need to look at what precipitated our actions, and treat ourselves with fairness. Too often, the people who fight back feel more guilty than the perpetrator who did the initial harming. Sometimes it is helpful to think about what a friend would say to us. It would probably be a realistic statement such as, "It wasn't *all* your fault." The harmful actions were brought on by harmful actions. Our behaviors were harmful, but not without cause, and we need to be compassionate rather than harsh and scolding when working with this type of guilt. If we are unable to do this, we may want to work with a therapist regarding the guilt that we are feeling.

- John shares:

    I still feel guilty about punching my dad, but he just kept badgering me about everything. It never stopped. One day, I lost control. I know what it means to lose your mind when you are in a rage because it happened to me. I should have walked away, but my rage took over and I punched him hard in the stomach and left. I took off in my car with the tires squealing and haven't seen him for three years. He thinks I'm a loser. But he's the only person that sets me off to the point of not being able to control myself.

Reasons for valid guilt might change as we grow in awareness

Years ago, people did not feel guilty throwing litter out of their car windows. Now, most of us dispose of our litter in appropriate ways. We have also grown in our awareness about smoking, and with this new awareness we are likely to feel guilty, knowing that we are not respecting ourselves or the people around us when we smoke. We may have felt guilty for thinking about leaving an abusive relationship and now, having grown in our awareness, feel guilty for *not* making the choice to leave, especially if we know that our children suffered. We may have resisted wearing seat belts, but now with our awareness, we buckle up to prevent the guilt that reminds us to take care of ourselves and our children. In the past, we may have felt guilty for playing, relaxing, or exercising, and now, after developing a greater awareness about our mental, emotional, and physical health, we feel guilty for *not* playing, relaxing, or exercising. If we view guilt as a friend, we realize that it offers healthy advice regarding our health, behaviors, relationships, and safety. We are also grateful that our guilt evolves as we evolve in consciousness. Like a good friend, healthy guilt does not abandon us but continues to give us gentle nudges that help us to achieve an emotionally balanced life.

Self-forgiveness and letting go of guilt

We may have harmed our children, partners, friends, coworkers, or parents. To the list of those we have harmed, we need to add ourselves. Our healing involves forgiving ourselves after we have made appropriate restitution and amends. In order to forgive ourselves in a healthy way, we cannot minimize nor can we exaggerate the mistake, harm, insensitivity, or other negative behaviors that caused harm. It may be more difficult to forgive ourselves than it is to ask for someone's forgiveness. There is a time to challenge ourselves to face up to the wrongs we have done and make amends. Having completed these actions, there comes a time to let go of the guilt, be gentle to ourselves, forgive, and avoid generalizing the guilt to all areas of life. As humans, we make mistakes, but we can resolve to not repeat the harmful behaviors. As our life unfolds, we will perhaps find other ways to make restitution to the people we have harmed.

> I need to forgive myself for…
>
> I can let go of the guilt because I have…
>
> My challenge:

Key Points:

1. Valid guilt is caused by behaviors that have involved verbal, physical, sexual, mental, or emotional abuse toward others or destruction of property.
2. The appropriate response to valid guilt is making amends, which involves taking full responsibility, recognizing the harm done to the victim, offering apologies, making restitution, and making an honest commitment to not repeat the harmful actions.
3. Guilt carries life-fostering messages when we experience survivor guilt, existential guilt, the guilt of self-betrayal, or the guilt that is felt when being irresponsible adults.

Chapter 9

Dealing with Irrational Guilt

    Unhealthy, toxic guilt is created by our *irrational thinking* and is detrimental to our emotional health. The definition of the word "irrational" in the Encarta Dictionary is: *Irrational (adjective) – Lacking in reason, contrary to logic.* When our guilt is contrary to logic, it is self-punishing because we feel guilty for no valid reasons. We feel flawed, unworthy, and innately *wrong*. Irrational guilt involves feeling responsible for things that are outside of our realm of responsibility, beyond our personal power, and expectations that we place on ourselves to be perfect. This type of guilt holds us hostage, negatively affects our emotional, physical, mental, and spiritual well-being, and sabotages our peace of mind.

    A healthy response to guilt is to analyze it to determine if the guilt is from harm that we have done to ourselves or others; false guilt taken on from people who are trying to control us; or irrational, toxic, neurotic guilt that we generate in our minds that needs to be dismissed. If we do not examine our guilt so that the irrational thoughts and beliefs are exposed, we continue to carry false and irrational guilt, unnecessarily.

◄ Anger and Guilt

Irrational guilt and relationships

Our irrational, toxic guilt is usually about a relationship with ourselves, our spouse, parents, children, or friendships.

- **Ourselves**: We may feel that we are inferior and inadequate and, as a result, feel guilty. Other reasons for feeling guilty may be for having negative thoughts, for making inadvertent mistakes, and for failing in our efforts of trying to be perfect. Persons who let themselves be doormats to others usually experience a high amount of irrational guilt.

- John shares:

    I can't remember any time that I felt good about myself and have felt guilty most of my life. I was raised in a really strict family, and I can't ever remember being told that I did something right or that I was good at anything. Now as an adult, I feel guilty for not wanting to go visit my family because it is still a hassle when I go there. They always ask the same questions, and I never have the right answers for them. I feel guilty when I don't make my sales quota at work. I feel guilty when I get depressed and can't function very well. I get down on myself and start thinking doom and gloom thoughts. Often, I feel guilty because I am not happy and grateful even though I have it pretty good.

- **Spouse**: We may feel guilty because we can't or don't always meet all of our partner's needs. Sometimes we think we don't love enough or spend enough time with our significant other and feel guilty. When there is conflict with our spouse and we express anger, even if we communicate our anger in a respectful and appropriate way, we may feel guilty.

- Mel shares:

    I know I don't meet all of her needs because she tells me that all of the time. I feel guilty when she says I don't care enough. Maybe she's right, or maybe I don't care in the exact way she wants me to care. I don't know. I'm confused. I try to be a good husband, but it seems like I can never do anything right. So the guilt is always there.

- **Parents**: We may feel that we should always please our parents, comply with their requests, take their advice, fix their relationship if it is dysfunctional, and not withhold information from them. We feel guilty when we leave home and our parents do not emotionally let go. When we think that we don't live up to our parents' expectations of us, we feel guilty.

- Sharon shares:

    I have tried hard to live up to my parents' expectations, but I'm never successful. I can't even buy my own car and think that I am making a good decision because my dad will always have another opinion. According to him, I buy the wrong things, pay too high of a price, or I buy what isn't necessary. So a lot of time I'm not honest with him because it's always a hassle. It feels like he doesn't want me around, but that I should always be around. This sounds a little crazy, but this is how I feel, and the guilt just never goes away.

- Kim shares:

    I have struggled with guilt most of my life. It's hard to live with myself. I think that I don't deserve to be successful, loved, or happy, and guilt is destroying my life. I felt guilty when I was a kid because I didn't get good grades like my older sister and wasn't as pretty. I did not feel loved and felt guilty because I really wanted my parents to love me.

- **Children:** As parents, we may feel guilty when we bring our children to day-care, when we don't spend enough quality time with our children, and because we are not always sure what to do in difficult situations with children. It's helpful to sort out our rational guilt from irrational guilt. Valid guilt prompts us to make changes, and the irrational guilt needs to be dismissed.

- Sally shares:

    It's the day-care drop-off that really makes me feel guilty because my son screams and throws a fit when I leave. It just tears me up, and it takes me half of the morning to get settled down again. It is absolutely the worst part of my day, and since I start work later than my husband, it's always me taking our son to day-care. So I live with day-care guilt. But we also need my income to live. I feel guilty working and I would feel guilty not working. I feel guilty when the house gets messy, and I feel guilty when I'm so tired, I don't even care about anything.

- **Friends:** We may feel guilty because we think we should always be available to our friends, despite busy schedules.

When we can't remove their pain and make their life better, we feel guilty. When our friends are unhappy and miserable, we may feel guilty for being happy and content.

- Sue shares:

    I have some friends who get together and complain about almost everything and everyone. It gets too depressing and I feel guilty for not wanting to be around them. I'm not sure I should be calling them friends, but I don't know how to stop being their friend because I don't want a big hassle. I've always been there when they needed me, but I'm getting drained. I want some friends that generate energy, rather than zap my energy. But I would have a lot of guilt if I left, so I guess I'll just hang on to my old friends.

Irrational guilt takes many forms

Guilt rooted in irrational thinking would be an endless list, but there are some common ways of thinking, if left unchallenged in our minds, that will result in false, toxic guilt. In the following examples of irrational guilt, notice the words: "should," "never," and "always." These words indicate irrational, toxic guilt. Also notice how often the toxic guilt is about being *perfect*. It is irrational to think we need to be perfect, and such a belief sets us up for failure and false guilt. We don't have to be perfect to be valuable! Joan Borysenko, a noted spiritual writer, describes toxic, irrational guilt: *In saying yes to guilt, we begin saying no to life.*

We can trace each guilt feeling back to the irrational thought or belief.

◂ Anger and Guilt

Irrational guilt with <u>myself</u>	**Irrational thought or belief**
Feeling guilty when I have been emotionally, physically, mentally, or sexually abused. Victims often take on the guilt that rightfully belongs to the perpetrator.	Irrational thought or belief: The abuse must have been my fault because I am inadequate and deserve to be punished.
Feeling guilty when I am not God-like: all-knowing, all-loving, all-forgiving, and able to do all things perfectly.	Irrational thought or belief: I should be able to be all-knowing, all-loving, all-forgiving, and do all things perfectly.
Feeling guilty for confronting abusive behaviors appropriately, but the abuser feels emotionally hurt when faced with the truth.	Irrational thought or belief: I should never confront because I might hurt someone's feelings.
Feeling guilty when I'm not successful at removing others' emotional pain and making them happy.	Irrational thought or belief: I should be able to solve all problems and make people happy.
Feeling guilty for making mistakes, even if they are small and natural.	Irrational thought or belief: I cannot make mistakes because mistakes are bad and reveal just how incompetent I really am.
Feeling guilty because I am trying to respond to too many unrealistic expectations from others, am not always successful, and I become exhausted.	Irrational thought or belief: I should be able to successfully do all things for everyone, and others are more important than me.

Feeling guilty because I am taking better care of myself, but now I feel like I am being selfish.	Irrational thought or belief: It is selfish to take care of myself.
Feeling guilty for being happy and positive when I am with people who are unhappy and negative.	Irrational thought or belief: I don't deserve to be happy, and I believe that suffering is more virtuous than being happy.
Feeling guilty for needing reasonable help at times from partners, family, friends, or colleagues.	Irrational thought or belief: I should be all-knowing, strong, and never need help.
Feeling guilty for not being able to quickly regain trust in someone who has hurt me or is untrustworthy.	Irrational thought or belief: I should always be trusting of others.
Feeling guilty when I cannot please an "impossible-to-please" person.	Irrational thought or belief: I should be able to do all things, even the impossible.
Feeling guilty because I feel different from other people.	Irrational thought or belief: It is bad to be different from others.
Feeling guilty because when I fail in one area of my life, I feel like a total failure.	Irrational thought or belief: I should be able to succeed in all areas of my life or I am a failure.
Feeling guilty when I don't want to go someplace, do something, or be with someone.	Irrational thought or belief: I should like everyone and always go along with their plans.

◄ Anger and Guilt

Feeling guilty for being angry, even though the anger is a response to being harmed.	Irrational thought or belief: I should never be angry.
Feeling guilty when saying "no!"	Irrational thought or belief: I am bad and selfish when I don't respond to everyone's requests.
Feeling guilty because I believe, "There is something wrong with me."	Irrational thought or belief: I'm not okay. There is something wrong with me.
Feeling guilty when controllers tell me that I *should* feel guilty, even though there has been no actual wrongdoing.	Irrational thought or belief: I should feel what people say I should feel.
Feeling guilty for taking the time to play and relax.	Irrational thought or belief: I am not worthy of taking time for myself.
Feeling guilty for spending money, even though it is for the necessities of life and the money is available.	Irrational thought or belief: I am not worthy and should not spend money, even for legitimate needs.
Feeling guilty for being sick, not recovering immediately, and having to take time off from work.	Irrational thought or belief: I should never be sick or take time off from work.
Feeling guilty when someone is overly kind or generous to me.	Irrational thought or belief: I do not deserve kindness from others.

Feeling guilty for not being attractive, handsome, slim, young, successful, intelligent, outgoing, a great cook, a great lover, a super dancer, a millionaire, the *perfect* wife, husband, friend, child, employer, employee, housecleaner, parent, athlete, or student.	Irrational thought or belief: I should be able to do all things perfectly, even the impossible.
Feeling guilty for being too tired to cook a meal and bringing home fast food, too tired to do the laundry, and falling asleep when I'm reading to my children at bedtime.	Irrational thought or belief: I should be able to do all things, for everyone, and never get tired.
Feeling guilty for having time conflicts, for not staying in constant contact with parents and friends, for the car breaking down, for my children falling down and hurting their knees at their friend's house, for working too much, for not working enough, for not exercising enough, for asking for help, and for receiving help when I ask for it.	Irrational thought or belief: I should be able to do all things, even the impossible, for everyone and do all things perfectly and never need help.
Feeling guilty for not feeling guilty.	Irrational thought or belief: Feeling guilty is virtuous and I should feel guilty.

Irrational guilt in <u>relationships</u>   Irrational thought or belief

Feeling guilty when I don't meet all of my partner's needs and wants.	Irrational thought or belief: I should be able to meet all of my partner's needs and wants.
Feeling guilty when I express feelings that displease my partner.	Irrational thought or belief: I should never express feelings that upset my partner.
Feeling guilty for not wanting to be sexual.	Irrational thought or belief: I should always want to be sexual when my partner does.
Feeling guilty for needing meaningful communication in a significant relationship.	Irrational thought or belief: I should have no needs in my relationships.
Feeling guilty when I am not heard or understood, even though I communicate clearly.	Irrational thought or belief: I should be able to make people listen and understand, even though they refuse to listen or distort what I say.
Feeling guilty for not caring for someone as much as a person cares for me.	Irrational thought or belief: I should be able to care as much as someone cares for me.
Feeling guilty for divorcing because the relationship is toxic.	Irrational thought or belief: I should be able to make a dysfunctional relationship work.
Feeling guilty for sharing the "family secrets"—the dysfunctional dynamics within a relationship—with a trusted person or therapist.	Irrational thought or belief: I should not discuss problems outside of the family.

Dealing with Irrational Guilt

Irrational guilt with <u>parents</u>	Irrational thought or belief
Feeling guilty because I never felt loved and couldn't make my parents love me.	Irrational thought or belief: I should have been able to make my parents love me.
Feeling guilty because when I was a child, I could not rescue myself or my family members from abuse.	Irrational thought or belief: Even though I was a child, I should have been able to rescue myself and family members from any type of abuse.
Feeling guilty when thinking that I'm not living up to my parents' expectations.	Irrational thought or belief: I should always live up to my parents' expectations, even the expectations I create in my mind that may not be true.
Feeling guilty when I do not want to be with parents every time I have vacation days.	Irrational thought or belief: I should always be with my parents whenever they want me to be with them.
Feeling guilty because I was not with a parent when he/she died.	Irrational thought or belief: I should be able to be in all places, at the exact right time.

Irrational guilt with children | **Irrational thought or belief**

Feeling guilty when my children make mistakes or misbehave.	Irrational thought or belief: If my children fail in any way, it's my fault.
Feeling guilty when I don't buy whatever my children want.	Irrational thought or belief: I should give my children everything that I didn't have as a child.
Feeling guilty when I take time to exercise, go to a support group, or have coffee with friends.	Irrational thought or belief: I don't deserve to take care of myself or relax.
Feeling guilty for not working outside of the home but also feeling guilty if working outside of the home.	Irrational thought or belief: I should not work outside the home and be with my children, but I should work outside of the home to earn an income.

Rational thoughts to correct irrational thoughts

- ❖ We are not God. We have limited powers and wisdom.
- ❖ We cannot correct a problem that is beyond our power, competency, and authority, or when we do not have the power to positively impact all of the reasons that create the problem.
- ❖ Doing our best is important, but we do not have to be perfect.
- ❖ It is not selfish to invest energies into taking care of ourselves.
- ❖ We cannot change other persons' behaviors or take away their pain. We can support their efforts toward healing and growth, but we can't do it *for* them.
- ❖ We have a right to refuse to be a puppet, servant,

over-functioner, or the only nurturer or communicator in a relationship.
- ❖ We have a right to confront a person who is emotionally abusing us, who makes us feel guilty as a way to control us, who controls with anger, or who badgers us into submission.
- ❖ We can choose to leave an abusive, toxic relationship that is unlikely to change. We can leave by emotionally detaching, or physically removing ourselves and our children.
- ❖ We do not have to feel guilty when we do not want to be sexual with our partner. We have a right to make choices about our physical body.
- ❖ We do not have to feel guilty for needing emotional intimacy in a primary relationship.
- ❖ We do not have to feel guilty for appropriately expressing our anger.
- ❖ We do not have to feel guilty if we have different interests, values, and priorities than our spouse or friends.
- ❖ We do not have to feel guilty if we share family problems with a safe person, therapist, or support group.
- ❖ For things we cannot change, we can do what we are able to do and turn the problem over to a Higher Power. The Serenity Prayer offers guidance: *God grant me the serenity to accept the things I cannot change, courage to change the things I can, and wisdom to know the difference.*

Steps to deal with *irrational* guilt

Dealing with our irrational, toxic guilt involves identifying the irrational thoughts and beliefs and replacing them with more rational, workable thoughts and beliefs. The steps in the process are:

◀ Anger and Guilt

1. Identify the irrational thought or belief that created the guilt.
2. Challenge the irrational thought and belief.
3. Replace the irrational thought or belief with a rational thought or belief.
4. Dismiss the irrational guilt.
5. Use positive affirmations to replace the irrational thought and belief.

Using positive affirmations

Affirmations are positive statements to replace irrational thoughts that create toxic guilt. Writing and repeating our own affirmations that are active and in the present moment can help us to reprogram our minds. Examples follow:

- ❖ I am able to identify the irrational thought when I feel irrational guilt.
- ❖ I have no need to punish myself with guilt.
- ❖ I can do my best but do not have to be perfect to be successful or happy.
- ❖ I can give up the belief that I have to *earn* love and self-esteem.
- ❖ I release my irrational guilt because it serves no healthy purpose for me.
- ❖ I am discarding any thought or belief that is life-diminishing.

> What irrational guilt am I carrying?
>
> What is the underlying irrational thought?
>
> What is a rational, logical thought?
>
> Do I need to modify the expectations I have for myself?
>
> Do I need to set limits on the expectations that others have of me?
>
> The guilt I have regarding my relationship is:
>
> In the past, my unhealthy ways of dealing with guilt were:
>
> What guilt can I dismiss and let go of?
>
> My affirmations to replace irrational thoughts or beliefs:
>
> Dealing with guilt in healthy ways, I expect to feel:

The guilt when ending a relationship

When a relationship or marriage ends, we may create guilt for ourselves by:

- ➢ Thinking that we should protect a partner from being emotionally hurt, even though we routinely experienced

⊰ Anger and Guilt

    emotional abuse in the relationship
- ➢ Thinking that others will view it as a personal failure if we leave a relationship
- ➢ Thinking that others have it worse and are being physically or sexually abused; therefore, our emotional pain must not be severe enough to end the relationship
- ➢ Thinking it is our responsibility to keep a relationship together, not recognizing that it takes two people to make a relationship function well
- ➢ Thinking that we should have done more, given more, and loved more when we were actually doing all that we could to make the relationship work
- ➢ Thinking that it is all our fault, when realistically it is not all our fault

Rational thoughts when ending a relationship

- We cannot protect a partner from hurt that has been created by her/himself.
- Other people may be abused more seriously than we are, but our emotional pain is real, needs to be acknowledged, and a plan of action needs to be implemented.
- One person cannot make a relationship work. It takes two healthy people to make a healthy relationship.
- We cannot allow our lives to be directed by other people's opinions.
- We probably tried many ways to make the dysfunctional relationship healthier. The person who feels guilty for leaving is often the person who put the most effort into making the relationship work.

When we are struggling in a dysfunctional relationship or

thinking about ending a primary relationship, we have to think rationally, because we are making serious decisions that affect our life and the lives of our children, if we have children. It is helpful to work with a therapist to explore all of the alternatives to divorce.

- Julie shares:

    I was accused of breaking up the family and felt guilty about that, but I just could not deal with his outbreaks of anger and sarcastic comments. Then I realized that I wasn't breaking up the family, but it was his behavior that really caused the relationship to fall apart. He made it impossible to stay and finally I said, "Enough is enough, I can't do this anymore and I can't stand by and watch our kids be frightened." So I didn't buy into his words when he said I was breaking up the family. I told him that he was the one that was responsible for our relationship coming to an end.

Key Points:

1. Unhealthy, irrational, toxic guilt is generated by irrational thoughts and beliefs that need to be replaced with rational thoughts regarding ourselves and our relationships.
2. *Rational* thoughts include: As humans, we have limited powers and wisdom. We cannot correct a problem that is beyond our power, competency, or authority or when we do not have the power to positively impact all of the causes that create the problem.
3. The steps to deal with irrational, toxic guilt are: identify the source of the guilt, identify the irrational thought and belief that create the guilt, challenge the irrational thought or belief, replace the irrational thought or belief with a rational thought or belief, dismiss the toxic guilt, and use positive

affirmations to replace irrational thoughts and beliefs.
4. *Rational thoughts* when ending a relationship include knowing that we cannot protect a partner from hurt that has been created by her/himself and that it takes two healthy people to make a healthy relationship.

Chapter 10

Strategies for Working with Guilt

The feeling and energy of guilt are different from anger. Anger usually *generates* energy and provides motivation to confront, make changes, or move on with our lives. Guilt, if not addressed, is more likely to exhaust our energy and lead us down the road of low self-esteem, depression, and feeling hopeless. The feelings of both anger and guilt, as well as other emotions, bring us information about ourselves or our relationships.

Too often, we do not realize that we are caught in a web of guilt, so we do not analyze our guilt to see if it is rational or irrational. We continue to do things out of guilt and obligation, rather than choice. We enable controllers' guilt-making tactics by allowing, accommodating, adjusting, complying, protecting, sacrificing preferences and dreams, and pretending that everything is fine when everything is not fine. If we do not refuse to take on the guilt that is projected on us by controllers or discard our irrational guilt, we are likely to accumulate a considerable amount of suppressed guilt, which adversely affects our mental, emotional, spiritual and physical well-being.

The first step in dealing with our guilt is to acknowledge it. Rather than resisting the feeling of guilt, or any other feeling, we invite it into our consciousness and listen to the message it brings.

◀ Anger and Guilt

Besides receiving information, when we recognize the feeling, embrace it, and claim it as our own, difficult feelings lose their power over us.

Crucial steps in working with guilt: prevention and intervention

Working with our guilt is a process that needs to start with ***prevention***. By being proactive, we can prevent many situations that cause valid guilt, guilt that is projected on us, or guilt that is self-created by our irrational thinking. When we discover ourselves to be submerged in guilt, we can do an ***intervention*** on ourselves and actively work with our guilt. By consistently implementing both prevention and intervention, we will experience less toxic guilt that usurps our energy and lowers our self-esteem.

Guilt <u>Prevention</u> Strategies

Design life with the Golden Rule — "Treat others as you would like to be treated." This will prevent guilt that is caused by behaviors that have harmed others.
Refrain from engaging in behaviors that are harmful to the self, such as being involved in addictive activities or abusing chemicals.
Be rational and reasonable with yourself to prevent unnecessary and invalid guilt.
Avoid the guilt of self-betrayal by being honest and refusing to sacrifice your beliefs and values to avoid conflict with others.
Develop strong personal boundaries so you do not internalize guilt that is projected on you, in attempts to control you.
Be a responsible adult rather than expecting others to compensate for what you do not do.
Treat yourself and other people with respect and compassion.

Take care of yourself mentally, emotionally, physically, and spiritually.
Refrain from bad-mouthing others, lying, spreading rumors, or seeking revenge.
Curb over-consuming that causes scarcity for others.
Realize that all people are interconnected and "what goes around, comes around." Our actions, whether supportive or abusive to others, will be returned to us in some form, at some point in time.
Continue to learn and grow, be all that you can be, and be grateful for your blessings.

Guilt **Intervention** Strategies

Make amends and correct the behaviors that cause harm to oneself or others.
Discard the guilt that is generated by irrational thoughts and beliefs.
Assertively confront the guilt and unrealistic expectations placed on you by controllers.
Refuse to be a martyr in relationships. Set limits if there are feelings of being unjustly treated.
Change negative attitudes into positive attitudes.
Share your resources with people less fortunate or people who are suffering from a natural or manmade disaster.

Strategies for working with guilt

Guilt Strategy 1: Increase your self-awareness by writing in a journal

Writing in a journal, drawing pictures, or creating diagrams are helpful ways to develop self-awareness and sort out healthy guilt from unhealthy guilt. If critical assessment indicates that the guilt is valid, appropriate actions need to be taken. If the guilt is toxic and irrational, the guilt needs to be removed from your thinking, which requires correcting your thought process each time you fall into the trap of irrational guilt. As your thinking becomes more rational, you will experience less toxic guilt.

If you are struggling with guilt, a simple way of identifying the cause of your guilt is to review the *prevention strategies* listed previously, to see where your guilt is coming from.

Guilt Strategy 2: Refuse to accept guilt projected by controllers

It's important to stay focused and not accept the guilt that is projected onto you in efforts to control you. Accepting guilt from others may not *feel* like a choice, but the reality is that *no one can make you feel guilty without your consent*. You make yourself a victim and offer guilt a permanent home when you take on guilt that controllers project on you. If you pay attention to your interactions with people, you will discover who manipulates you with guilt in attempts to control you. These are the people that you are tempted to be dishonest with, or are actually dishonest by making false excuses to avoid being with them or doing things for them.

Once you realize that guilt is a way to control, you can prepare yourself ahead of time and keep your guard up when you interact with controllers who use guilt to manipulate. When you need to be in conversations with them, you can remain calm and disregard negative or controlling guilt statements. By staying alert and listening closely to the conversation, you can avoid being sucked in to manipulative tactics that feign weakness or helplessness. Rather than enabling the guilt that is used to control, you can confront guilt messages or choose to not associate with controlling guilt-makers. If you cannot escape a guilt-maker because she/he is your spouse or parent, you can emotionally detach. Disengagement or detachment is not abandonment of the controlling person. Rather, it is refusing to be manipulated by controlling behaviors.

Detachment is:

- ➢ Stepping back and not internalizing guilt-making statements
- ➢ Maintaining your personal boundaries and not giving away your personal power
- ➢ Refusing to have moods, thoughts, or choices change because of a controller's guilt statements
- ➢ Refusing to internalize blame and unjust criticisms
- ➢ Refusing to act out of guilt, fear, or insecurity
- ➢ Refusing to believe that taking care of the self and setting personal limits is selfish

When you detach, you are taking care of yourself and honoring the life that has been given to you. If you are planning to stay in a controlling relationship and stay healthy yourself, detaching is crucial. Emotionally detaching from a controller is not a total solution but does reduce the stress of getting caught up in manipulative guilt. Be prepared for controllers to get upset and escalate their control when you stop complying with their requests.

Guilt Strategy 3: Work the steps to deal with <u>irrational</u> guilt

1. Identify the irrational thought and belief that create the guilt
2. Challenge the irrational thought and belief
3. Replace the irrational thought or belief with a rational thought or belief
4. Dismiss the guilt
5. Use positive affirmations to replace the irrational thought and belief

Guilt Strategy 4: Talk out your guilt with a person that you trust

It is helpful to talk to a trusted friend or an emotionally safe person. You may have branded yourself as innately flawed and feel guilty, but if you share your thoughts and feelings with someone, you are likely to discover that many of your thoughts and beliefs are irrational or saturated with false information. Ask for honest feedback about the validity of your guilt. If you are feeling guilty because of an irrational belief like "I feel guilty when I make mistakes and don't do it perfectly," your friend will probably point out the irrational thought, and tell you to dismiss it. If you would rather not talk directly to a good friend, you can speculate what a friend would tell you, which is likely to be more objective and rational than you are with yourself. Or, you may decide to start professional therapy if you feel that you need help in dealing with your guilt. A good therapist can help you sort out your guilt and take the necessary actions.

Guilt Strategy 5: Talk out your irrational guilt in privacy

In a private and comfortable place, talk out your toxic guilt. You may want to talk loudly and emphasize certain words. Allowing yourself to feel and express your feelings is far healthier than suppressing your guilt. Use your body and voice to perform a serious or humorous performance, and exaggerate the guilt. When you hear your guilt in words, combined with body movement, you will be more able to understand how you take on the guilt from others, or how you create guilt by your irrational thoughts and beliefs.

Guilt Strategy 6: Visualize the person who manipulates with guilt and talk to her/him.

If you are not comfortable speaking directly to a person who manipulates you with guilt, you can imagine the person sitting in an empty chair. Say all of the things that you would like to say about being controlled through guilt. Stand up to feel more powerful as you speak to the imaginary person in the chair. Let all of your feelings out, without minimizing the hurt and anger that you feel. This is also an effective rehearsal if you decide to actually speak to the person about the manipulative guilt messages that are used to control you.

Guilt Strategy 7: Self-advocate by directly confronting the person who projects guilt on you

Refuse to be a hostage to toxic guilt. When you are being controlled by guilt, it is best to speak up, even though it may be easier to remain quiet. Speak to the person with "I" statements. For example, you can say, "I feel like you are trying to control me with guilt." You need to be credible when confronting and use a calm voice. Confronting the controller is an attempt to end the dysfunction and prevent future situations where guilt is used as a control tactic.

- Know and respect your personal boundaries and learn

Anger and Guilt

- boundary language, such as saying "no," or, "I can't agree to that." Or, "I have a conflict with the time." Or, "I feel that talking to you will not result in a positive outcome." Say these statements without feeling guilty.
- Just because someone tries to put us in a one-down, inferior position doesn't mean we have to go there, unless there is a safety issue.
- Be okay with the controller's disapproval when you start setting limits.
- Don't feel guilty when making healthy choices regarding your own life.
- Take care of yourself without feeling selfish or guilty.

Guilt Strategy 8: Share your guilt in a Twelve-Step or other type of support group

The Twelve-Step program offers a spiritual way to live and a safe place to express feelings, including guilt. Participating in a recovery group may be your first experience with people openly expressing their feelings. Recovery groups are safe places to express your guilt because you will not be judged, criticized, or shamed. The program has a step-by-step process to deal with the guilt that is caused by actual wrongdoing. Healing happens in Twelve-Step groups as evidenced by members' positive behavior and attitude changes. Making amends is a part of recovery, in addition to expressing gratitude for the many blessings in life. If Twelve-Step groups do not interest you, there may be support groups offered at your place of worship or counseling agencies in your community that can help you deal with guilt feelings and difficult situations in your life.

Guilt Strategy 9: Use mental imagery, visualizing toxic guilt leaving your body

Relax your body by breathing deeply. Visualize the toxic guilt leaving your mind, emotions, and body as you exhale. Inhale positive, pure energy coming into your body, replacing the toxic air.

Guilt Strategy 10: Use positive affirmations to replace toxic guilt

Affirmations strengthen your resolutions regarding toxic guilt. Writing your own affirmations is more powerful because they will be specific to your experiences.

- I recognize the difference between wrongdoing, rational guilt, and false, irrational guilt.
- I reject invalid, manipulative guilt used to control me.
- I think clearly and refuse to punish myself with irrational guilt.
- I have a right to set limits for myself.
- I am competent, confident, and supportive of myself.
- I do not accept guilt that doesn't belong to me.
- I do not enable controlling behaviors.
- I do not generate guilt for myself by my irrational thinking and beliefs.
- Today I choose thoughts that are supportive and nourishing.
- My life keeps getting better and better.

Guilt Strategy 11: Forgive yourself after you have made sincere amends

Hanging on to guilt long after you have made sincere amends can be self-punishing and detrimental to your emotional health. In some situations, it may be nearly impossible to forgive yourself if you have seriously hurt someone who will suffer the rest of their lives. However, with many other types of less traumatic harmful actions, forgiving yourself after making amends and moving on with a productive, caring, and purposeful life will demonstrate that your amends and promises to change behaviors are sincere.

Guilt Strategy 12: Discover other creative guilt strategies

You can discover other creative ways to work with your guilt, knowing that by addressing the various forms of guilt and taking appropriate action, you will create a healthier life on all dimensions of mind, body, emotions, and spirit.

Key Points:

1. Working with guilt is a process involving both prevention and intervention.
2. Guilt strategies to work with toxic guilt include:
   - Talking with a trusted friend or therapist about your guilt.
   - Verbalizing your guilt in privacy and creating a dramatic performance
   - Self-advocating by confronting the person who projects guilt on you
   - Working with your guilt in a support group
   - Mentally imagining the guilt leaving your body
   - Using positive affirmations

Chapter 11

Guilt Our Friend

Thinking that guilt can be our friend seems to be an unusual way of viewing this emotion. However, it is true that guilt can be our ally, rather than our enemy. The feeling of guilt, similar to anger, is purposeful because it alerts us to some aspect about our life that needs to be changed. By listening to our valid guilt and taking action regarding the message our guilt brings, we will discover that guilt is not a foe but an emotion that gently guides us as we travel through life.

Guilt is our friend…

- ❖ When guilt alerts us to actual wrongdoing and prompts us to make amends
- ❖ When guilt signals to us that we're not living up to our own standards and reasonable expectations of ourselves
- ❖ When guilt alerts us that we are taking on the guilt projected by controllers
- ❖ When guilt provides a way of feeling good about ourselves because we are taking positive action
- ❖ When guilt encourages us to consider the needs of others and be more caring

◄ Anger and Guilt

- ❖ When guilt sends a message to take our share of responsibility when we are involved in relationship problems
- ❖ When guilt is a motivator to change unhealthy or addictive behaviors that negatively affect ourselves and others
- ❖ When the discomfort of guilt helps us to learn from negative experiences, so we are less apt to repeat mistakes
- ❖ When guilt alerts us to our faulty ways of thinking that need changing to be more reality-based and life-fostering
- ❖ When guilt reminds us to be more honest with ourselves and others
- ❖ When guilt prompts us to help disadvantaged people and disaster victims in whatever way that we are able
- ❖ When our guilt directs us to prevent future regrets by choosing to be with someone who is difficult, but may only be with us for a short period of time
- ❖ When our guilt signals us to think about a decision that might be wrong, too extravagant, unfair, or self-indulgent at the expense of others
- ❖ When our guilt prompts us to respect and honor our self and stand by our moral and ethical principles.

Similarities between guilt and anger

Anger and guilt are normal feelings that are often misunderstood, avoided, or expressed inappropriately. Both emotions can be our foes or friends. Anger and guilt are foes if they are used to control others or expressed in ways that are harmful. Both emotions can be our friends because they carry messages to us regarding ourselves or our relationships. Both anger and guilt can be signals that something is wrong, that we are behaving or thinking irrationally, or that we are being controlled by someone. Both feelings can motivate us to change unhealthy behaviors so that we make better choices and behave in ways that are consistently more effective, positive, and in alignment with our beliefs and values. If we can develop a good relationship with our anger and guilt and learn skills for dealing with these emotions, we will reduce our stress, feel more emotionally balanced, and have a better relationship with ourselves and with others.

Key Points:

1. Guilt is our friend when it signals to us that we're not living up to our own standards and expectations of ourselves and is a motivator to make amends for hurtful actions.
2. Guilt reminds us:
    - to be respectful of others
    - to share our caring feelings
    - to take care of ourselves physically, mentally, emotionally, and spiritually
    - to be grateful for having a high quality of life
3. Valid guilt prompts us to confront wrongful actions, respect and honor our self and all others, stand by our moral and ethical principles, recognize the interconnectedness of all people, have a purpose in life, and take personal responsibility for making a positive contribution to the world.

Chapter 12

Being Proactive with Anger and Guilt

Being proactive is making conscious choices and taking actions that eliminate problems *before* they occur. Life poses many situations where we can be either proactive or reactive. When we are proactive, we plan ahead, take responsibility, and implement a plan. When we are reactive, we respond to others with inappropriate expressions of anger. And/or we continue to live with toxic guilt that we accept from others or generate by our irrational thinking.

There are three *powerful* ways to be proactive:

I.   Focus on prevention and intervention
II.   Change irrational thinking
III.   Stay in the center

By being diligent in using these three strategies, our lives will change from being reactive and thinking and behaving in the same self-sabotaging ways; to being *proactive* and making conscious decisions about our actions. When we are proactive, we take charge of our lives and take responsibility for the way we think and the way we act.

◀ Anger and Guilt

I. *Focus on prevention and intervention*

These strategies, along with your creative ideas when working with yourself, are proactive and result in reducing the type of anger and guilt that is detrimental to our lives.

Anger <u>prevention</u> strategies

- ❖ Realize that anger is a feeling, and feelings are neither good nor evil.
- ❖ Be knowledgeable about anger and take responsibility for how your anger is expressed. If it is suppressed, you are harming yourself. If anger is expressed aggressively, it is abusive to others and destroys relationships.
- ❖ Be aware of irrational thoughts and beliefs that create unnecessary anger. Become more self-disciplined and positive with your thinking.
- ❖ Deal with problems when they are still manageable, rather than letting them accumulate, which increases the chances of having a blowup or meltdown.
- ❖ Work through past anger so it doesn't infuse angry emotions into current situations.
- ❖ Learn to be assertive, rather than passive, passive-aggressive, or aggressive when expressing your anger.
- ❖ Prevent anger by giving up the need to control others.
- ❖ Prevent anger by giving up the need to be the center of attention.
- ❖ Prevent anger by reducing the amount of time spent with toxic persons.
- ❖ Eliminate viewing television violence or playing violent video games.
- ❖ Learn to set limits to prevent over-extension, which is an

Being Proactive with Anger and Guilt

- effective way to take better care of yourself.
- Be proactive and decide what situations need to be addressed, and what situations can be dismissed as unimportant.
- Release your personal anger in safe ways, which helps you to be more rational when you are experiencing challenging situations in relationships.
- Never make problems larger than they need to be.
- Don't expect other people, especially children, to have the same timetable or priorities as you do.
- Have correct information and be sure to understand the background and context of a situation before becoming angry about an issue.
- Make sure that expectations of others are reasonable.
- If sarcasm underlies a person's statement, ignore or confront the sarcasm.
- Ignore minor irritations.
- Remind yourself that:
    » You have no right to control others.
    » Compromise is not defeat.
    » Other people have a right to disagree.
    » People may not love, care, and support you in ways you would like them to.
- Refuse to internalize destructive criticism and view it as truth.
- Change negative attitudes into positive attitudes.

Guilt <u>Prevention</u> Strategies

- Design life with the Golden Rule—"Treat others as you would like to be treated." This will prevent guilt that is caused by behaviors that have harmed others.

◀ Anger and Guilt

- ❖ Refrain from engaging in behaviors that are harmful to the self, such as being involved in addictive activities or abusing chemicals.
- ❖ Be rational and reasonable with yourself to prevent unnecessary and invalid guilt.
- ❖ Avoid the guilt of self-betrayal by being honest and refusing to sacrifice your beliefs and values to avoid conflict with others.
- ❖ Develop strong personal boundaries so you do not internalize guilt that is projected on you, in attempts to control you.
- ❖ Be a responsible adult rather than expecting others to compensate for what you do not do.
- ❖ Treat yourself and other people with respect and compassion.
- ❖ Take care of yourself mentally, emotionally, physically, and spiritually.
- ❖ Refrain from bad-mouthing others, lying, spreading rumors, or seeking revenge.
- ❖ Curb over-consuming that causes scarcity for others.
- ❖ Realize that all people are interconnected and "what goes around, comes around." Our actions, whether supportive or abusive to others, will be returned to us in some form, at some point in time.
- ❖ Continue to learn and grow, be all that you can be, and be grateful for your blessings.

Anger **Intervention** Strategies

- ❖ Stop, think, and make a conscious choice whether a situation needs to be addressed or whether it can be dismissed. Take a time-out and breathe deeply. If the anger is too intense, take time to walk, exercise, or talk with a trusted friend before expressing the anger to the person involved.

- Use calming and rational self-talk so that you can think more clearly about what action is most appropriate to the situation.
- Be assertive, which is being honest, open, and respectful of others.
- Express anger only when you are calm enough to communicate effectively and appropriately.
- Recognize the anger that is generated by irrational thoughts and make the necessary and positive changes in the way you are thinking.
- Set personal limits when necessary and say "no" in appropriate ways.
- Self-challenge with "Am I making this a bigger deal than it needs to be?"
- View the problem objectively and approach it rationally, step by step.
- Change negative attitudes into positive attitudes.

Guilt <u>Intervention</u> Strategies

- Make amends and correct the behaviors that cause harm to oneself or others.
- Discard the guilt that is generated by irrational thoughts and beliefs.
- Assertively confront the guilt and unrealistic expectations placed on you by controllers.
- Refuse to be a martyr in relationships. Set limits if there are feelings of being unjustly treated.
- Change negative attitudes into positive attitudes.
- Share your resources with people less fortunate or people who are suffering from a natural or manmade disaster.

II. Change irrational thinking

Anger generated by irrational thoughts and beliefs

We generate anger for ourselves by our irrational thinking, such as:

- ✓ I should be able to change the behaviors of another person, and I get angry when they don't change.
- ✓ People should respond to my requests immediately, and if they don't, I have a right to be angry.
- ✓ I want to be the center of attention, and when I am not, I get angry.
- ✓ The worst things always happen to me, and I'm angry a lot of the time.
- ✓ People are out to get whatever they can from me. I always end up being taken advantage of, and I get angry.
- ✓ I'm angry inside but never let it out because I don't want to look bad.
- ✓ People should think like I think, and when they don't, I get angry.
- ✓ When I fail in one area of my life, I am a total failure and I get angry at myself.
- ✓ Other people *make* my life miserable, and I get angry.
- ✓ It's not my fault, and I can't help it if I get angry.
- ✓ I am helpless, weak, inadequate, vulnerable, powerless, and angry.

Guilt generated by irrational thoughts and beliefs

There are common ways of thinking, if left unchallenged in our minds that result in false, toxic guilt. The words "should," "never," and "always" indicate irrational, toxic guilt as well as the guilt we generate when we aren't able to be *perfect*. Toxic guilt adversely affects our relationships with ourselves and others, and includes such thoughts and beliefs such as:

- ✓ Feeling guilty when I have been emotionally, physically, mentally, or sexually abused. Victims often take on the guilt that rightfully belongs to the perpetrator.
- ✓ Feeling guilty when I am not God-like: all-knowing, all-loving, all-forgiving, and able to do all things perfectly.
- ✓ Feeling guilty when I'm not successful at removing others' emotional pain and making them happy.
- ✓ Feeling guilty when I cannot please an "impossible-to-please" person.
- ✓ Feeling guilty for not being attractive, handsome, slim, young, successful, intelligent, outgoing, a great cook, a great lover, a super dancer, a millionaire, the *perfect* wife, husband, friend, child, employer, employee, house-cleaner, parent, athlete, or student.

Changing our irrational thinking reduces anger and toxic guilt

Thoughts and beliefs create our perceptions and feelings, including anger and guilt. Changing our irrational thoughts and beliefs involves the following process:

1. Identify the thought or belief.
2. Challenge the thought or belief:
    - ✓ Is there any basis in reality to support this thought or belief as being true?
    - ✓ Does this thought or belief have words such as "never" or "always"? If so, it probably is irrational, exaggerated, or false.
    - ✓ Is this thought or belief life-fostering or life-diminishing?
    - ✓ Is this thought or belief fear-based?
3. If the thought or belief is determined to be irrational and

life-diminishing, dismiss the thought.
4. Create a realistic thought or belief to replace the irrational thought or belief.
5. Continue life with the new thought or belief. When other irrational thoughts or beliefs occur, use this same process. If you are diligent in refining your thoughts and beliefs, you will discover that the frequency of your irrational thoughts or beliefs decreases, which means you are creating less anger and guilt for yourself.

Changing our irrational thinking is an effective strategy for prevention of anger and guilt problems. We are the creators of our irrational beliefs. No one else is responsible for the emotional turmoil we feel because of our irrational ways of thinking.

III. Stay in the center

In our society, many people express anger and guilt in the extremes. The goal in developing life skills for personal empowerment is to stay in the center—the "golden mean" as Aristotle, the famous Greek philosopher, taught around 350 BC.

Anger - Stay in the center

| Anger is suppressed or expressed in ways that are indirect and manipulative. | **Anger is communicated in direct, honest, and respectful ways.** | Anger is directed outwardly in aggressive ways that harm others verbally or physically. |

Emotional health requires that we be in the center and express our anger *assertively*. Rather than suppressing, or having our anger come out sideways and manipulative, we express our anger in honest and respectful ways, using normal voice tones, speaking directly to the person about the specific issue. We stay in the center and confront with confidence, kindness, and consideration for ourselves and for the other person.

Guilt — Stay in the center

The guilt is not acknowledged.	**The guilt is acknowledged and responded to in healthy and responsible ways.**	**The guilt is excessive.**
These people feel they have no reason to feel guilty and do not take responsibility for their hurtful behaviors that are harmful to themselves or others.	These people make mistakes and take responsibility, but reject unrealistic, irrational, or excessive guilt. They refuse to take on guilt that is directed toward them by controllers.	These people feel guilty too frequently and are not aware of how they accept toxic guilt from others and generate their own guilt by irrational thinking.
Action Taken: These people seldom make amends because there is an unwillingness to admit fault.	Action Taken: These people readily make amends when they have harmed someone.	Action Taken: These people apologize too frequently, and often for no valid reason.

◄ Anger and Guilt

If we stay in the center, the cause of guilt is determined and action is taken. We do not deny our guilt, nor feel guilty when we have done nothing wrong. When there is actual wrongdoing, amends are made. Manipulative, controlling guilt messages are rejected and are often confronted. Irrational guilt is dismissed. Staying in the center position involves clear thinking, honesty, and responding to *valid* guilt in responsible and appropriate ways.

Being proactive rather than reactive is a major shift in consciousness and positively changes lives. Many strategies for dealing with anger and guilt have been offered in this book, but these are three of the most powerful approaches to use when dealing with difficult aspects of anger and guilt.

Having freed ourselves from thinking that anger and guilt are our enemies, we can increasingly recognize that anger and guilt are emotions which can be our loyal and trustworthy friends.

Hopefully, this book has started the process of looking at both anger and guilt as emotions that can be viewed as friends, rather than enemies that sabotage our lives. Dealing with these emotions and working with them will result in a higher quality life on all of the dimensions of mind/body/spirit and in your relationships. May God bless you on your journey toward greater health, enriched relationships, and living out the meaning and purpose in your life.

Bibliography

AA World Services, Inc. *The Twelve Steps and Twelve Traditions*, 2002

Columbia Pictures, *...And Justice for All,* 1979

**Check my website for empowerment strategies:
carolrogne.com**

Also By Carol Rogne

One Canoe, Many Paddles

Healing and Living Our Spirit

    A crucial step in our healing involves removing harmful false beliefs, resentments, and ways of thinking that are negative, fear-based, and limited.

    Having removed what is sabotaging our lives, we can then create a life with more positive ways of thinking, behaving and relating. This will enable us to move closer to optimal health on all levels of our being: the mental, emotional, spiritual and physical.

    One Canoe, Many Paddles – Healing and Living our Spirit, describes the personal growth journey and offers life skills and spiritual principles, including those in the Twelve Step Program, to express, celebrate and live our spirit with gratitude.

Learn more at:
www.outskirtspress.com/onecanoemanypaddles

Also By Carol Rogne

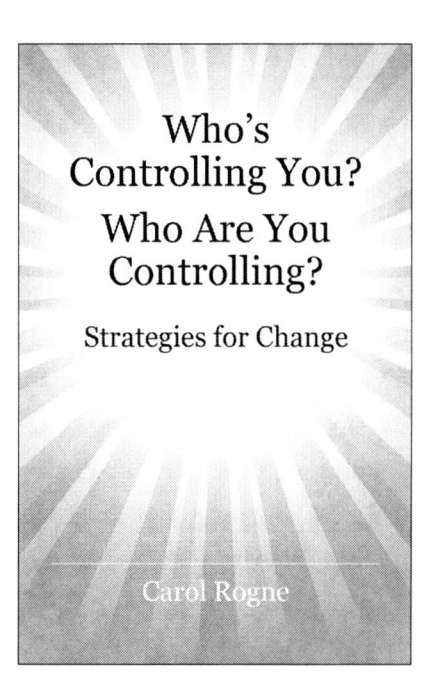

Who's Controlling You? Who Are You Controlling? Strategies for Change

Who's Controlling You? Who Are You Controlling? -

Strategies for Change

Considered one of the best books ever written on power used to control others, this book defines emotional and mental control as interpersonal violence that creates trauma in the emotional lives of adults and children.

You will be empowered by the topics:

- The many ways that power is used to control others.
- Characteristics of controllers and the people they control.

- Strategies for positive change:
- Protecting ourselves from emotional abuse.
- Confronting, rather than enabling controllers' manipulative, life-diminishing tactics.
- Re-claiming and designing our life based on personal choices, values, beliefs and goals.
- Surrendering controlling behaviors if we are controlling others.
- Restoring relationships damaged by controlling behaviors.

We can recover from the emotional devastation of being controlled. Our empowerment journey will result in becoming a healthy person and parent. Being empowered, we can bring the message to others, including the next generation, that we all have certain rights, among them being, "life, liberty, and the pursuit of happiness."

Learn more at:
www.outskirtspress.com/whoiscontrollingyou

FEB 2 0 2013

CPSIA information can be obtained at www.ICGtesting.com
Printed in the USA
LVOW121300101011
249834LV00001B/1/P

9 781432 777579